Sausalito Wooden Boat Tour

Welcome to the third edition of the Sausalito Wooden Boat Tour, a self-guided tour of the historic Sausalito waterfront and the eclectic collection of wooden boats and historic vessels that call this little village their home.

Some of the people and boats you will encounter on this tour have lived adventurous seafaring lives; others have never navigated beyond the Golden Gate. Nonetheless, the handcrafted wooden boats that grace our harbors continue to inspire adventure, art, poetry, and song in those who know and love them. Whether your appreciation is based on the historical or artistic significance of wooden boats, or is simply a reflection of your own personal experience, it is my hope that the Sausalito Wooden Boat Tour brings you a little bit closer to the nautical life with a renewed appreciation for all things made with the hand, eye, and heart.

Victoria Colella
Author / Founder
Sausalito Wooden Boat Tour

Acknowledgements

The first edition of this book was made possible through the support and sponsorship of the Richardson's Bay Maritime Association.

The mission of the Richardson's Bay Maritime Association (RBMA) is to promote and publicize the maritime history and traditions of Richardson's Bay, and to serve as a public resource for maritime exhibits, learning, and research activities. (www.rbma.net).

Thank you to all my friends and neighbors on the Sausalito waterfront who contributed to this project.

A fond farewell to the late, great Charlie Merrill, Phil Frank and Harold Sommer, Ale Ekstrom and Larry Moyer — miss you!

Resource information is from the Arques School of Traditional Boatbuilding, Bay Model Visitor's Center, Bear Boat Association, Bird Boat Association, City of Sausalito, Classic Yacht Association, Floating Homes Association, Golden Gate Tall Ships Society, Master Mariners Benevolent Association, Richardson's Bay Maritime Association, San Francisco Maritime Museum, Sausalito Historical Society, Sausalito Public Library, Spaulding Wooden Boat Center, West Marine.

PARTICIPATING BUSINESS SPONSORS
Valhalla Signworks

The Sausalito Wooden Boat Tour
First Edition October 16, 2003
Second Edition June 10, 2004
Third Edition April 22, 2014
Third Edition, 2nd printing, March 2015
Third Edition, 3rd printing, April 2016

Printed by DiggyPod

ISBN 978-0-615-98054-6

Preliminary edits by Sam Berry and Jessica Christiansen

Sausalito Wooden Boat Tour

Guided Tours Available

www.sausalitowoodenboattour.com

This book is dedicated to all
who own and care for wooden boats—
especially on the Sausalito waterfront.

After the last Ice Age, the glaciers melted, and for thousands of years the waters from the great inland lakes flowed back to the ocean through an opening in the coastal hills we know as the Golden Gate. And for thousands of years the Coastal Miwok people lived in peace and harmony along these shores. Why not? They had everything they needed. Water, wood, fish and game were plentiful. Sausalito, from the Spanish Saucelito, translates to "little willow." Seven sister streams flowed down from the hills and everywhere the fresh water hit the Bay, the willows would grow. So the pirates, the whalers, the merchants coming in from the ocean looking for fresh water would look for the willows.

For hundreds of years, the Spanish galleons perused the California coastline propagating their missions. They never noticed the Golden Gate because it was mostly enshrouded in fog. Until one day in 1775, Lieutenant Juan Manuel de Ayala, aboard a wooden bark *San Carlos*, thought he saw something. He sent in a few men to investigate. Three days went by, and they did not return. Ayala had to go looking for them. Can you imagine entering this bay for the first time—the pristine beauty? Would you want to leave? Well, they didn't either. Ayala found them camped out on the northwest side of Angel Island in a place now known as Ayala Cove.

In 1823, San Francisco's first port captain William Richardson arrived aboard the wooden merchant ship *Orion*. He was first mate and a very clever fellow. He took one look at the area and jumped ship to become San Francisco's first port captain. He took one look at San Francisco and realized it was nothing but a bunch of sand dunes, so he pitched his tent on the north side of the Golden Gate in Sausalito. Richardson knew that every ship that came into port would have to buy water, wood, and supplies, and he was going to be the one to sell them these goods.

Richardson was not so interested in building a town as he was an empire. He married the daughter of Don Ignacio, the Presidio Commander, and acquired 20,000 acres of land he called “El Rancho del Saucelito”. Just about everything you can see — Mount Tamalpais to Angel Island, around and back—was his.

Richardson was doing pretty well, but he didn't figure on a couple things— the Bear Flag Rebellion and the California Gold Rush. When the gold miners descended from all over the world, they anchored their ships in the middle of the Bay, and headed for the gold in "them thar hills." On the way they took all the water, wood, and food they wanted without paying Richardson for any of it. Richardson died a broken man chasing money and lawyers, but we did name the stretch of water along Sausalito's coastline Richardson's Bay.

SAUSALITO HISTORICAL SOCIETY

A federally designated anchorage, Richardson's Bay offers safe harbor with direct access to San Francisco Bay and the Pacific Ocean, making it a favorite port for day sailors and world cruisers alike.

Why is this called the Sausalito Wooden Boat Tour?

You can't really talk about Sausalito's nautical history without talking about wooden boats. Wooden boats have been built on the Sausalito waterfront as long as there have been people on the waterfront. The Coastal Miwoks were building the equivalent of sit-on-top kayaks out of tule reeds. Other local tribes built dugout canoes. San Francisco's first port captain William Richardson taught these same natives how to sail and build and repair wooden boats in the European tradition. This tradition has carried forward to this day.

Through the late 1800s and early 1900s, the Sausalito waterfront was dotted with fishermen and wooden boat builders. Mostly they built work boats, service boats and tug boats like the 1938 45-foot *Telco* now in the San Francisco Maritime National Historical Park or the wooden sub-chasers built by Madden & Lewis during World War Two (WWII). They also built classic yachts and recreational day sailors such as the Bear Boats, Bird Boats, Golden Gates, Hurricanes, Clippers, and Mercuries.

During prohibition, wooden boat builders were building rum runners, fast little boats with secret liquor compartments that would zip out three miles to hook up with the mother ships from Canada and Mexico. Meanwhile, right next to them, the boat builders would be fixing up the Coast Guard boats to catch the rum runners!

PERMISSION OF LUTHER GREEN

Actor Errol Flynn's Zaca *is the largest and perhaps the most famous wooden boat ever built in Sausalito. Built in 1930 by the Nunes Brothers Boat & Ways Co., this John Alden designed 118-foot gaff-rigged schooner, was originally commissioned by Templeton Crocker. Restored in 1993,* Zaca *remains one of the finest classic yachts in the world today.*

During World War Two (WWII) Libertyships were built here. These ships were steel, but their lifeboats were wood as were the subchasers and barges being built for the war effort. This activity served to bolster the wooden boat industry in Sausalito, but after WWII there was a decline. By 1960, most boaters wanted fiberglass boats. Thanks to the vision of two men— Donlon Arques and Myron Spaulding—Sausalito retained its wooden boat focus and became the mecca for wooden boat building in California.

The wooden boat building activities have been fortified over the decades with Spaulding Wooden Boat Center and Arques School of Traditional Boatbuilding taking the lead. The building of the Mathew Turner Educational Tall Ship and A Sausalito Community Boating Center at Cass Marina are also underway. There are historic restorations such as the 1885 *Freda* and the Charles Van Damme Paddlewheel & Steamstack

Restoration Project. The older houseboats and floating homes also serve to protect and preserve our maritime treasures by incorporating wooden boats and historic vessels into their construction.

Wooden boats are celebrated at the annual Wooden Boat Show at the Corinthian Yacht Club in Tiburon. Classic sailing yachts gracefully traverse the Bay with races and regattas organized by the Master Mariners Benevolent Association (www.mastermariners.org).

PHOTO BY ERIK SIMONSON

The Master Mariners Benevolent Association (MMBA) was originally established in 1869 to help families who had lost loved ones at sea.

This symbol identifies members of the MMBA.

The tour begins on the north end of Sausalito at Kappas Marina, which is located in back of the Harbor Center at the intersection of Bridgeway and Gate 6 Road. You can drive or bike there directly or take a taxi or bus from downtown Sausalito (North Bay Taxi, 415.332.2200). Please be sensitive to and respectful of the people and neighborhoods. Stay on the main docks and do not knock on doors, peek in windows, or step aboard a boat without a personal invitation from the owner. Explore and enjoy, but most of all, respect the ambiance of the waterfront.

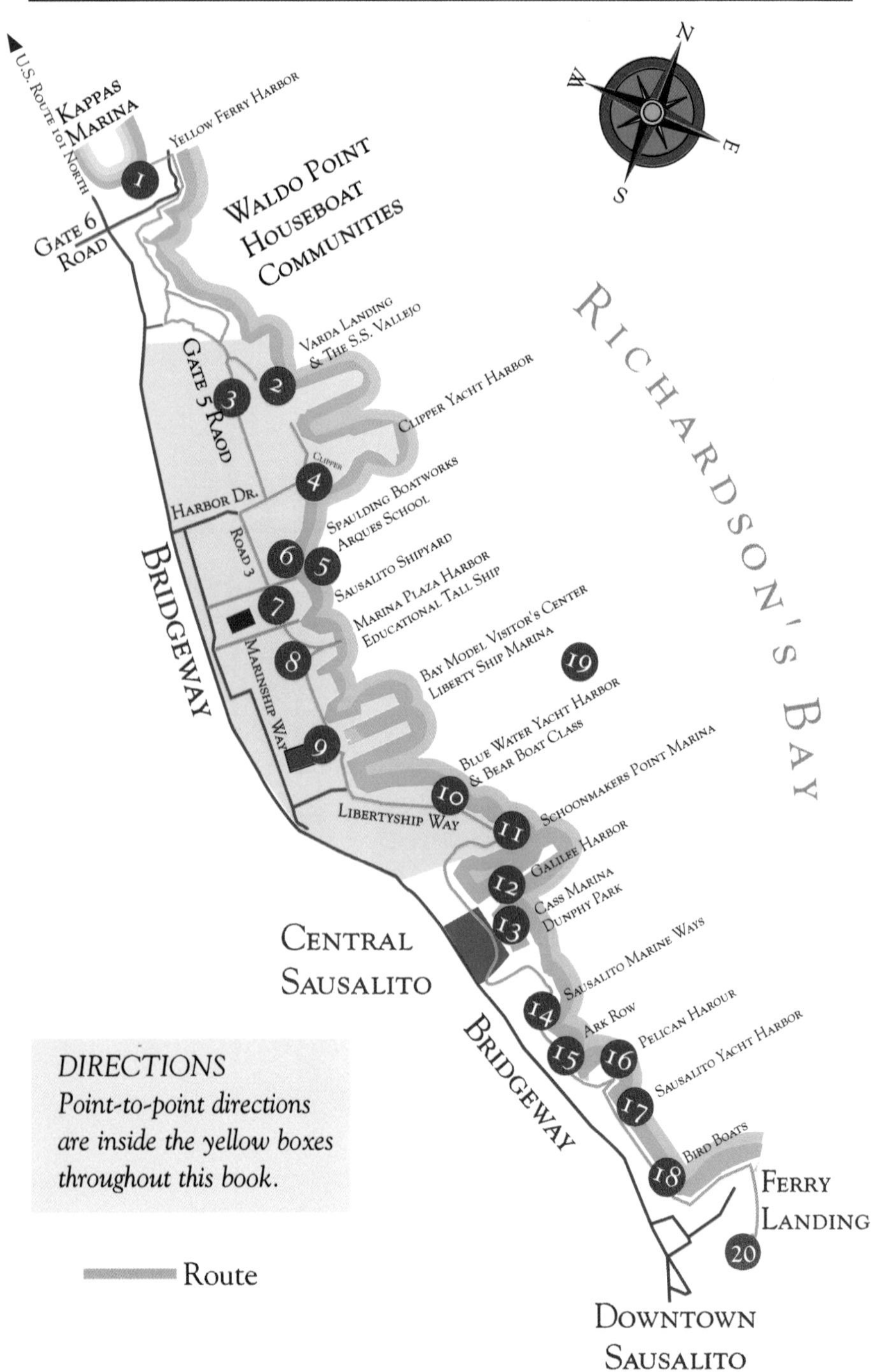

DIRECTIONS
Point-to-point directions are inside the yellow boxes throughout this book.

Route

Table of Contents With Map Key

For decades the houseboats at Kappas Marina were considered illegally docked, but this dispute was resolved by Senator Carol Migden in 2006.

Overlooking the floating community of Kappas Marina from the adjacent park, our "Sleeping Lady", Mount Tamalpais, dominates the skyline. Her reflection in the water is a familiar and comforting sight to locals and visitors alike.

Once a free-floating community of funky houseboats, the "Last Free Ride" is long past, and berth spaces are now considered prime real estate with prices to match. Like floating condominiums, the new communities are all hooked up properly with electrical, phone, internet, cable and sewage. But in the beginning, it was not this way. In the beginning, if your boat was offshore 100 yards, the only way to get to it was to take a plank and move it from boat to boat until you reached your boat. There were no docks. Hundreds of people lived here wild and free before the Waldo Point development began in the 1970s.

Original houseboater Chuck Green recalls that one of the first things the developers did was to install the pilings for A Dock. Chuck and his buddy didn't like it. They went out in the middle of the night with rubber gators and a two-man logging saw, and they cut down the newly placed pilings. They were very proud of themselves until they discovered that the sawing action had corkscrewed them into the bay mud, and they couldn't get out! The morning construction crew arrived to find the pilings down and two sets of rubber gators stuck in the mud.

Throughout the 1970s and 1980s, the area painfully went through a complete rebuilding era resulting in what you see today. Highlighted in this section are a few favorites— the older vessels with stories to tell.

In 1967, Ken Gutelben purchased a 1940s steel lifeboat for $200 from Matson Steam Ship Company in New Jersey and converted it into a houseboat for $2,000. He lived on her in the Barndale Marina in Alameda and rediscovered the boat in 2012 as a participant on the Sausalito Wooden Boat Tour!

Gutelben's lifeboat now sits atop a boat-shaped concrete barge. Most of the new homes now float on concrete barges. These barges are hollow, serving as storage or second level living space.

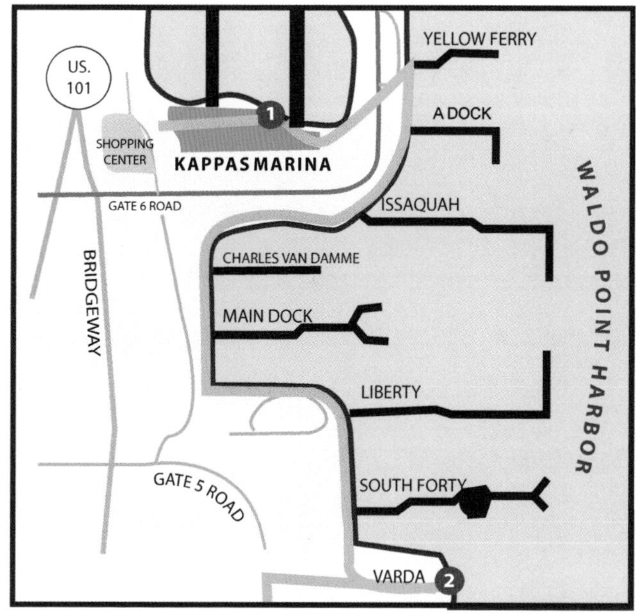

DOCK MAP

As you enter Gate 6 Road from Bridgeway, turn left behind the shopping center at One Gate 6 Road. Immediately on your right through the gate is Kappas Marina and park.

As you pass through Kappas Marina, head for the water across the street and turn left into Yellow Ferry Harbor, home to the City of Seattle Ferry *or* Yellow Ferry (*www.yellowferry.com*).

Yellow Ferry's wooden hull rotted away and she was placed upon a new concrete barge, doubling her size and making her the largest houseboat in Sausalito.

Jean Varda's graphic greets visitors.

This 1888 121-foot side-wheeler was built in Portland, Oregon and is the oldest surviving wooden-hulled ferry on the West Coast. She provided the first regularly scheduled ferry service on Puget Sound, and in 1913, became the first steamer for the Martinez-Benecia line. During WWII, she was requisitioned by the United States government for the Mare Island run. The Tellis family brought her to Sausalito in 1959, where she has enjoyed regular care ever since. In fact, the entire Yellow Ferry Harbor was built around her.

Inside Yellow Ferry: The bohemian vibe runs deep.

What's the difference between a houseboat and a floating home?

A houseboat was once a boat that someone turned into a home. A floating home was never a boat but rather a box on a barge of some kind. The original floating homes were called "arks" because they rise and fall with the tide like Noah's Ark. You will encounter a few of our surviving arks on this tour.

As you enter the dock at Yellow Ferry, you will immediately see two great examples of a floating home and a houseboat.

Floating Home–The Clamshell

A 1970s style floating home, this classic is way ahead of her time—created with 100% recycled materials. If you look closely, you will see barn wood from Marin, Victorian windows, church doors and other found objects.

Historic Houseboat WWII Balloon Barrage Barge

This historic houseboat was made from a decommissioned WWII balloon barge. These boats, with their massive iron hulls, were built in Sausalito and used as anti-aircraft devices. They would surround an area, such as the Golden Gate Bridge, and then run steel cables hundreds of feet in the air using balloons. An enemy aircraft approaching at night, could not see the cables and their wings would be cut off—low tech, but effective!

From Yellow Ferry follow the sea wall south to A Dock.

A DOCK

Fruit and Vegetable Barge

This historic wooden barge used to transport fresh produce from the Delta to Bay Area towns. After a fire, she was placed atop a new concrete barge. Another piece of local maritime history preserved!

From A Dock, follow the sea wall south to Issaquah Dock.

ISSAQUAH DOCK

This dock is named after the *Issaquah* ferryboat, a 1914 Lake Washington steam ferry. She ended up here as home to the early houseboaters and was demolished in the 1980s. Only her wheelhouses were saved, which now serve as the entrance to Galilee Harbor.

UNIVERSITY OF WASHINGTON LIBRARIES. SPECIAL COLLECTIONS DIVISION. NEGATIVE # UW7816

Feng Shui on the Docks

Feng shui is about the harmonic balance of energies. Imagine you are out in the middle of the ocean. All that water... all that sky... But where is your connection to the land? It's the wood in your hull! That's why a fiberglass boat can never replace a wooden boat. Energetically, it does not have the goods. People who live on houseboats or floating homes have the same issue, no land. But the folks on Issaquah Dock have a beautiful solution: Behold the gardens of Issaquah!

Community Gardens at Issaquah

If the houseboat communities are about anything, they are about freedom of expression—permission to be different. Here, this spirit is reflected in the gardens as well as the homes.

The Pirate

This 1910 steam powered tugboat ran on the Sacramento Delta and San Francisco Bay until it was converted to a houseboat in the 1930s. When Sterling Hayden lived aboard, he modified the transom exterior to look more like a riverboat.

Hollywood actor, adventurer, sailor, father, writer

Sterling Hayden made the front page of the *New York Times* when he absconded with his four children against court orders and headed for Tahiti on his sailboat *Wanderer*. In his best-selling book, also titled "Wanderer," Sterling states "Voyaging belongs to seamen, and to the wanderers of the world who cannot, or will not, fit in. If you are contemplating a voyage and you have the means, abandon the venture until your fortunes change. Only then will you know what the sea is all about." Sterling also described Sausalito as "the gem in the crown of the USA."

South around the bend will be a new park at the corner of Gate 6 and Bridgeway (may still be under construction)

Ground Zero–Where The Houseboat Communities Began
Arques Salvage Yard, Charles Van Damme Ferryboat and Houseboat Wars

SAUSALITO HISTORICAL SOCIETY

Under the new park at Gate 6 Road, lies the wooden hull of the famed 1916 Charles Van Damme (CVD) ferryboat. The CVD was the first car ferry built for service from Richmond to San Rafael and was destined to become central to Marin County's maritime, music, and houseboat history.

In 1960, on three high tides, Donlon Arques pulled the CVD ferryboat up onto the mud flats in his salvage yard and Juanita Musson opened Juanita's Galley. "Eat it or wear it" was her motto. She was tough on the adults but loved kids and kept a menagerie of animals down below in the hull.

In 1968, Marty Martinez opened a fancy nightclub on the CVD called The Ark. Coincidentally, we had a nationally-renowned recording studio in Sausalito called the Record Plant. In between sets, these recording artists were hanging out in The Ark. Suddenly, we were listening to some of the top music talent of the era. When the folks from the city found out about it, they were here in their top hats and tails, mink coats, and high heels. One day Marty looked around and decided this was not a great place for a fancy nightclub. The bohemians had moved in from San Francisco's North Beach. They took parts and pieces of anything they could find in Donlon's salvage yard, put them together, and called it home. There were hundreds of people floating wild and free and Donlon was letting them do it. He was the father of the houseboat communities!

After the nightclub closed, the CVD was offered to the city of Sausalito as a library. The city turned it down. It was at this point that the rag-tag floating community made it their clubhouse. For $2 on a Friday or

Saturday night you could have all the beer you could drink and dance all night to the famed Joe Tate & the Redlegs band. Tate found himself in the middle of the houseboat wars.

When the county moved in with demolition permits, the community fought back. There was a huge public outcry, and the folks at Gate 6 won the right to stay there and live as they wished.

In 1983, the CVD ferry was bulldozed, but one of the iconic paddle wheels and steam-stack remained for decades. Her story continues to educate and inspire all.

Supporters removed the 1916-artifacts and are working to restore and exhibit the paddle wheel and steam stack in the new park.
www.CharlesVanDammeFerry.org

The Gates Cooperative–The Last Vestige of the Original Houseboat Community

With the reconfiguration of Waldo Point comes big changes for the Gates community. The 36+ boats here will be redistributed either among existing docks or clustered together at their new floating dock just south of the new park. The new dock will be appropriately named *Charles Van Damme*.

Follow the waterfront south past the park. Between The African Queen *and the original arks will be the new* Charles Van Damme *dock.*

African Queen

The pile driver used to build the Carquinez railroad bridge sat upon this wooden barge (down below). The barge was later used by the Morton Salt Company and sold to its current owner and resident by Donlon Arques in 1959.

Original Floating Homes

Arks first made their appearance in the late 1800s. They were kept in the Belvedere Lagoon in winter and towed into Richardson's Bay in summer as vacation homes for the city folk. Parties aboard an ark were usually accompanied with music and fireworks. Arks were very popular after the 1906 Earthquake, there were hundreds of them, now only a few originals remain (See more on Ark Row, page 56).

Ark de Triumph

Originally named ArkElig, *this is actually three arks put together. Once owned by a public relations consultant for the Barnum & Bailey Circus.*

The Mayflower–Circa 1907

Built by Anderson & Cristofani in San Francisco, this is best example of an original ark that we have in Sausalito. She retains her wooden hull with metal towing irons, redwood walls, arched roof, and a balcony that almost entirely encircles the house. Mayflower *was placed onto pilings between 1920 and 1930. Sausalito's four-term mayor, Robin Sweeny, lived here for decades. The Mayflower changed hands in 2016.*

MAIN DOCK *First dock after the arks*

Sittin' in the morning sun
I'll be sittin' when the evening comes
Watching the ships roll in
And I watch them roll away again.
–Otis Redding

Main Dock is the oldest dock; it was built before WWII. Otis Redding was inspired to write *Dock of the Bay* on a houseboat here in 1967, Main Dock being the only existing dock at that time. The song was completed by guitarist Steve Crooper who released it after Redding's death.

Apoplexy *floats on her original wooden hull.*

Apoplexy

Once featured on the TV program "Bay Area Backroads," *this 1943 Higgins LVCP was converted to a houseboat in 1968. These landing craft were credited as "the boats that won the war." The resident artisan has lived here since 1978.*

Dorado

Tucked between the docks is Shoshana's wooden sid skiff built by Ray Speck in 1977.

Ark Pickleweed

This 1900 original floating home lives to tell the wild and decadent tales of houseboat life in the 1960s. Photographer-lawyer for the arts, Albert Morse, lived aboard with Christine Valenza (Art for Change). Morse once defended R. Crumb and published the book "The Tattooists."

LIBERTY DOCK

Stay close to the edge of the path, turn left onto the walkway leading to Liberty Dock.

Evil Eye

This WWII balloon barge transformed into a houseboat in the 1960s. It was home to famed author Shel Silverstein. Shel's friend, Larry Moyer, lived here with his wife Daine until he passed away in the spring of 2016. Evil Eye continues to be part of the Silverstein Trust.

There's too many kids in this tub
There's too many elbows to scrub
I just washed a behind
That I'm sure wasn't mine
There's too many kids in this tub
- Shel Silverstein

Dorathea

This 1907 flat-bottomed tugboat was built to haul hay on the Sacramento River. Her rustic wooden hull was put on a concrete boat-shaped barge in the 1990s to keep the vessel intact.

Sand Barge

This home was built on top of a sand barge. Barges like this were used to haul sand during the construction of U.S. Route 101 in the late 1930s.

SOUTH FORTY PIER

Stay close to the water's edge and traverse the wooden boardwalk over to South Forty Pier—Home of the Grand Dames

South Forty Pier was the last pier to be developed by Waldo Point Corporation and residents designed their own docks. Ramps from the main dock lead to communal pods. There is also a large gathering area in the middle of the dock. These features are unique to South Forty Pier.

The Owl

Chris Roberts built his home over the top of a pile driver with the help of Skip Melcher and friends in the 1970s. Skip recalls, "We just started at the top and worked down, with no plan and a lot of drugs. When we finished we looked up and said, 'Oh, it's an owl'. So we named it the Owl." More of a sculpture than a house, she stands as a testament to the creative spirit that brought the original houseboat communities into existence. Her current owner has provided for this grand dame since the 1980s, exemplifying good stewardship — a true waterfront hero!

Becky Thatcher

To the left of the South Forty entrance is a an original floating ark built in the early 1900s. A rich redwood interior was created by Chris Roberts in the 1960s. This is home to Sausalito's own Tom Sawyer, Joe Tate and his wife Donna.

Idylboot

The Tates keep Ale Ekstrom's boat close and safe.

Lone Star

This WWII landing craft houseboat has retained many of her historic elements: She is sitting on her original wooden hull, the patio was once the platform where the troops disembarked, and the hardware used to raise and lower the platform is still attached.

Mirene

This 1912 64-foot tuboat is owned by Ryan Phelan and Stewart Brand, a former "Merry Prankster" and founder of such visionary endeavors as the Whole Earth Catalog *and* The Well. *The table upon which Otis Redding wrote the song "Dock of the Bay" lives inside* Mirene *(www. mirenetugboat.com).*

S.S. Maggie

This massively built 1889 steam schooner was retired from light cargo duty in the 1930s. Her ribs are 8-10 inches thick and her planks are 3-4 inches thick and double planked! Now, safe on a boat shaped barge and beautifully restored. (www.ssmaggie.com)

Her massive hull shows through below in the V berth.

Mariposa

If this boat looks a bit Chinese, it's because she has the hull of a Chinese shrimp junk buried in her concrete barge. When she's lit up at night, the Mariposa takes on the appearance of a Chinese lantern.

Train Wreck

A pullman train car from the 1889 Northwestern Pacific Railway has been split in two and each section placed at a 90-degree angle. In between them, an elegant home was built. This gives the appearance of a train intersecting a house. In the barge below is the master bedroom and up above the bed you can see the cables and gear boxes, which have been left intact.

PHOTO BY GARY FERBER

2 Varda Landing and the S.S. Vallejo

At Gate 5 Road, turn left and stay on the same side of the street for about 20 feet and then turn left into Varda Landing.
Head for the water between these two buildings. On your way, dance, sing, recite and make merry as you call up the spirit of Varda!

Jean Varda

SAUSALITO HISTORICAL SOCIETY

Jean Varda (1893-1971) was an adventurer, an expatriate Greek boat builder, theatrical set designer, and collagist who studied in Paris with artists such as Braque and Picasso. He danced with Nijinski in the Imperial Royal Ballet in London and developed his own color theory while creating a new style of mural painting with tiles and mirrors. Varda lived on the *Vallejo* from 1949-1970. His ashes were carried off to sea with much fanfare aboard a brightly painted felucca fishing boat.

S.S. Vallejo Ferryboat

The Vallejo *ferryboat was reborn in 2000 after extensive renovations at the hands of the* Vallejo *Corporation. In 2012, she was fitted with a new hull. The golden pyramid over her name board is a gift from the Crowned Prince of Tonga and, so it seems, her international relations continue to keep the vibe alive.*

To Have Faith is to Trust Yourself to the Water. Faith is a state of openess or trust.

Vallejo's rich history makes it the most famous boat on the waterfront. Launched in 1879 under the name *Oregon & California Railroad*, her steel hull was prefabricated in Philadelphia and shipped around Cape Horn for assembly in Portland, Oregon. She served as a passenger ferry crossing the Willamette River until 1889.

In 1892, the vessel was moved to San Francisco and renamed *Vallejo*. The opening of the Golden Gate Bridge in 1937 marked the decline of the ferryboat era and, by 1947, the *Vallejo* was sold for scrap and ended up in Donlon Arques' salvage yard in Sausalito.

Of course, Donlon did not destroy the boat. Instead, he sold her in 1949 to Jean Varda, artist Gordon Onslow Ford, and architect Forest Wright. The "anchor outs" and the waterfront community gravitated towards the *Vallejo* and the so called "beatnik" era began.

Besides being a home to Varda, Zen Buddist philosopher Alan Watts and writer Jack Kerouac lived aboard. One night in a drunken stupor, Kerouac built a property fence down the middle of *Vallejo* to keep Alan Watts off his side. Watts, upset with a painter who overcharged him, stood on the top deck in full ceremonial garb and shot arrows at the painter. Renowned for its parties, *Vallejo* became a catalyst for new ideas.

SAUSALITO HISTORICAL SOCIETY

In 1967, Alan Watts, founder of the *Society for Contemplative Philosophy*, brought together the *The Houseboat Summit* with Timothy Leary, Allen Ginsberg, Gary Snyder, and Alan Watts to discuss LSD.

In 1971, Jean Varda dies of a heart attack as he disembarks from a plane in Mexico City. In 1973, Alan Watts unexpectedly died in his sleep on *Vallejo*. In 1978, Saul Rouda produced a film entitled "*The Last Free Ride*," a reenactment of the houseboat wars that took place at Waldo Point a few years prior. The interior of *Vallejo* was used for the interior dance sceenes. This film has become a Sausalito cult classic!

At this point, Vallejo is almost 100 years old and deteriorating rapidly. Over the next 22 years, many people try many different schemes to keep the Vallejo intact. But it was the Vallejo Corporation that saved the day!

But to me nothing - the negative, the empty - is exceedingly powerful. - Alan Watts

3 Marinship Historic District - Gate 5 Road

Head inland through the parking lot to Gate 5 Road. Cross the road, but take note that this is not just any road. This is Gate 5 Road, and this was the assembly line for the big ships. Under the pavement lie the gantry crane rails.

The entire country was taken by surprise when the Japanese bombed Pearl Harbor in December of 1941. With the advent of WWII, there was a sudden need to quickly rebuild our fleet and Sausalito was chosen as one of the ideal sites for a shipyard. The W.A. Bechtel Corporation, acting with the authority of the U.S. government, acquired the necessary land for the proposed six launching ways and shipyard. Bechtel Corporation and Cal Ship were responsible for the Marinship.

In March 1942, 15 days after Sausalito was chosen as the site, excavation of beautiful Pine Point neighborhood began. Thirty to forty homes and buildings were moved or torn down. In order to fill the mud flats of Richardson's Bay, 838,763 cubic yards of earth and rock were moved from Pine Point, Waldo Point, and surrounding areas. Some 26,000 pilings were driven to support all of the buildings and shipways.

A deepwater ship channel 300 feet wide and one and a half miles long, required three million cubic yards of bay mud to be dredged. The shipyard buildings were still under construction when the first keel was laid for the Libertyship *William A. Richardson* in June 1942. The Liberty ships were built to send food and supplies to the United Kingdom and by December 1942, seven ships had been launched.

In June 1945, Marinship set a world record by constructing and delivering the oiler *Huntington Hills* in just 33 days. These oilers were 550-feet long and, with a combination steam and electric engine, they could move through the water at 23 knots. By the end of World War II, Marinship had constructed 15 Liberty ships, 16 fleet oilers and 62 tankers, a monumental 93 vessels in three and a half years.

SAUSALITO HISTORICAL SOCIETY

Seventy thousand people worked day and night to build the ships that won the war!

Thirty-five percent of the workforce were woman. John Pullum, who worked in the yards, remarked that "the woman were better welders than the men because they could follow instructions!"

BY S. FERGOSON, MARCH 1944, THE MARIN-ER NEV

An astonishing 838,763 cubic yards of earth and rock were blasted from Pine Point, and 26,000 pilings driven to form the Marinship district. This forever changed the character of the little fishing village. Our working waterfront now includes industrial and creative uses that would have otherwise vanished if not for restrictive zoning in the Marinship district.

SAUSALITO HISTORICAL SOCIETY

SAUSALITO HISTORICAL SOCIETY

The William A. Richardson *was the first of the Liberty Ships built in 1942.*

SAUSALITO HISTORICAL SOCIETY

SAUSALITO HISTORICAL SOCIETY

Buildings on Gate 5 Road During WWII

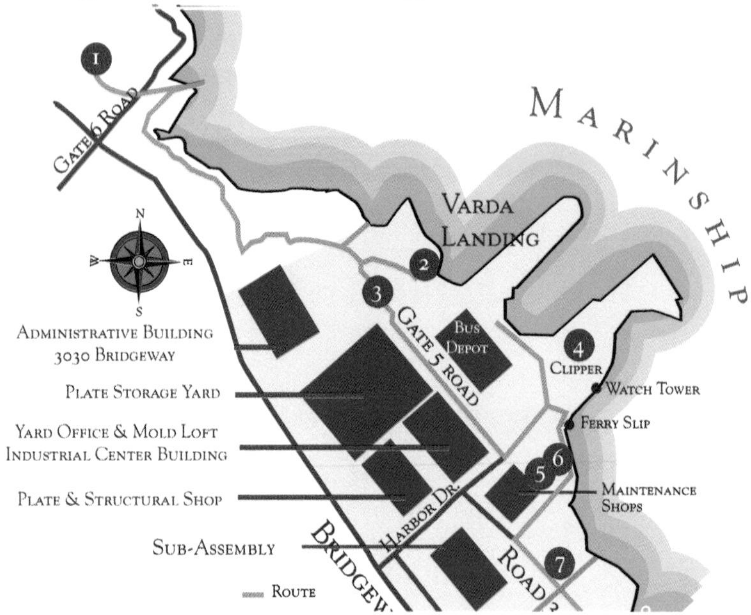

Several of the buildings that existed during the Marinship years are still in use today. The Industrial Center Building (ICB), 3030 Bridgeway, The Bay Model Visitor's Center and the Sausalito Shipyard *ways are a few of the more prominent structures, but there are many other smaller WWII structures along the waterfront that provide workspace for maritime crafts people and related industries.*

Plywood patterns for the ships' hulls were fabricated on the top floor of the Industrial Center Building (ICB), then carried to the plate and structural shop for production. These and other prefabricated parts were then taken to the sub-assembly building. Here, all the pieces were unitized into one section of the big ship. These sections were then transported by the gantry cranes to the shipways on Road 3 for installation. Once the heavy work was finished, the ships were moved to the outfitting docks (in front of the Bay Model) for completion.

Workers were enticed from the deep south by higher wages ($1.20 per hour versus $.35 per hour in other parts of the country). Thirty five percent of the workforce were women. Across the Bay where the Troop ships were being built worked "*Rosie the Riveter.*" Here we had "*Wendy the Welder.*"

Continue along Gate 5 Road towards Harbor Drive.

3030 Bridgeway–*Marinship administrative headquarters during WWII.*

Heath Ceramics–*In 1944 Edith Kiertzner Heath's one-woman ceramic exhibition at San Francisco's Palace of the Legion of Honor launched her and her husband into their own ceramic business. This building has served as Heath's corporate headquarters, factory, and showroom since 1956. Step inside to view their award-winning dinnerware and architectural tile. Edith's original casting molds are still in use today.*

Industrial Center Building (ICB)–*The top floor of this WWII building was the mold loft. One open-span, it allowed for the ship's plans to be layed out and patterns cut. The size of the building, therefore, approximates the actual size of the big ships.*

Famous American Expressionist, Walter Kuhlman, was the first artist to open a studio here in 1956. Kuhlman was part of the Sausalito Six. Richard Diebenkorn was one of the six. These were the Jackson Pollocks of the West Coast. The place has been filled with artists ever since. (www.icbartists.com).

Clipper Yacht Harbor

Turn left on Harbor Drive and walk one block towards the water and through the gates of Clipper Yacht Harbor. Once inside the gate, turn right towards the water.

This Clipper One, *built by Myron Spaulding, was the first of 20 Clipper sailboats commissioned by Cliff Pederson to race against the Nunes Brother's Mercury boats.*

During the Marinship years, the present Clipper Yacht Harbor was a bus depot. The land was acquired after WWII by Liberty Ship captain Cliff Pederson. Today, Clipper Yacht Harbor is a "tip top" marina offering a variety of family activities, bay cruises, day fishing, and hosts several maritime businesses.

PHOTO BY JAN PEHRSON

Sports Fishing Pier . *Mural artist, Victoria Colella helps Harold Sommer teach his grandson, Andy "The Ropes."*

Harold Sommer was a tugboat captain famous for restoring the *Wander Bird*, a German pilot schooner originally named *Elbe* 5. She made an historic passage around Cape Horn in 1936 with Irving Johnson at the helm, and Warwick Thomkins, Sr. who wrote about his account in the book, "*Fifty South to Fifty South*."

Sommer found the *Wander Bird* languishing in the mud flats of Richardson's Bay and enlisted folks along the waterfront to pitch in time, money and materials. Fully restored, she now resides at the Maritime Museum in Hamburg, Germany. Sommer was also an accomplished artist noted for his detailed oil studies of tugboats in action.

Go to the far left of the main gate.

KKMI–Kaplan Marin

To the far left of the main gate is KKMI boat yard. A massive rectangular steel lift with the KKMI logo on the side is visible. Do not get too close to the operations but notice all the different hull shapes on the boats that have been lifted out of the water and are awaiting their turn in the yard. KKMI works on everything from world-class yachts to old wooden fishing boats and demonstrates leadership in upholding environmental standards.

Santana 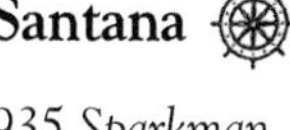

Humphrey Bogart's 1935 Sparkman & Stephens schooner, Santana, *on the Master Mariners race course, with the Kaplan family at the helm*

PERMISSION OF PAUL KAPLAN

From the Clipper mural site, follow the water past Fish restaurant and turn left. "Spaulding Boatworks" is visible on the building in front of you.

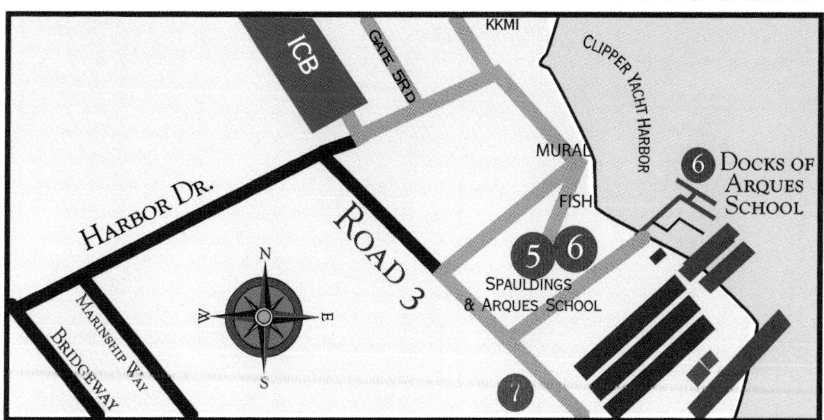

Permission of Spaulding Center.

Myron Spaulding was a living legend and acclaimed yachtsman. Prior to establishing his own boatworks, in 1943, he worked at the Madden & Lewis Company. He designed his own yacht class called Spaulding 33 as well as a class called Clipper, of which he built 70. Some of the most famous of Spaulding's boats are the *Buoyant Gal*, *Swami*, and the *Chrysophyle*. Spaulding sailed in six TransPacific Yacht Races, and in 1936, swept nearly all of the prizes aboard the Sparkman & Stephens yacht *Dorade*. Spaulding was passionate about boats but made his livelihood as the second violinist in the San Francisco Symphony. He also played professionally with the vaudeville house orchestras and movie houses accompanying the silent films of the era.

The Spaulding Boatworks was built in 1951 and is considered to be the "Cathedral of Wooden Boat Building" in California. There are several things happening here: A community-based museum quality restortion of *Freda*, the Youth and Adult Boat Building and Apprenticeship Programs, and a full service marine center. The inclusion of the Arques School of Traditional Boat Building completes Myron's vision. The marine center's new director, Bill Edinger, welcomes visitors and is working to create a museum and library to enhance their experience.

Freda

The Freda *has been widely celebrated as the "Matriarch of San Francisco Bay." A 32-foot gaff sloop, she was built in 1885 and is the oldest active sailing yacht on the West Coast. After a meticulous eight year restoration under the direction of Robert Darr, Freda was launched in April 2014. Here she makes her debut at the 2014 Master Mariners Wooden Boat Show in Tiburon.*

Community Boat Launch

The newly renovated crain can lift up to 12 tons. Gathering for a wooden boat launch is just one of the many events hosted by Spauldings. (www.spauldingcenter.org)

This sleek strip-planked canoe was created in a few weeks by a small team of dedicated young people participaing in the after-school program.

Dixie

PHOTO FROM SPAULDING WEBSITE

This adorable Casco Bay lobster boat serves as the Center's tour boat.

Avatar–The Spaulding 16

The Youth Boatbuilding and Apprenticeship Program summer students built this wooden lapstrake boat, a design that Myron envisioned as a young man. The students chose a recycled wind surfing rig instead of a traditional rig, otherwise the boat was built using traditional methods.

PHOTO BY ALBERT MORSE

Donlon Arques envisioned "a school and center for the restoration and replication of small wooden boats that have had historical significance in the greater San Francisco Bay area." In 1996, his vision was fulfilled when Robert Darr, a master boatbuilder, designer, and teacher, founded the Arques School of Traditional Boatbuilding with an endowment from the Arques Foundation.

The Arques School is located inside Spaulding Wooden Boat Center. It is a small school dedicated to teaching the art of building wooden boats using traditional methods and materials. They focus on the use of hand tools, harvest their own woods, and stay clear of toxic materials. Darr teaches students patience and persistence in learning this complex craft. The Arques collection of wooden boats speaks for itself. Each beautiful work of art teaches a different lesson of purpose, design, and construction.

2016 marks the 20 year anniversay of the Arques School!

"You never get tired of looking at a wooden boat. It's more alive, ever changing. The wood breathes and shifts, changes shape… and that's OK," says Darr.

Eleanor

Double-ended 21-foot Marconi sloop is constructed with planks on sawn and bent frames. Black locust wood is used at the bow and stern, as it is rot resistant.

Head inland from Spauldings and make a left on Road 3 into the Sausalito Shipyard & Marina (old Arques).

Sausalito Shipyard & Marina, the former Arques Shipyard, is where the WWII Liberty ships were assembled and launched. The original shipways are still in use today. This is where we haul out the fire boats, ferry boats, floating homes, house-boats and classic yachts.

The *Arques School of Traditional Boat Building* was located here from 1996 until 2007, and most of the wooden boat shops in this area were established by graduates of the school. The bigger boat yards like *Bayside Boatworks*, *Aqua Maison* and *Richardson Bay Boatworks and Ways* keep Sausalito's maritime industry strong.

Inside the shipyard are a host of maritime craftspeople and related services. Riggers, divers, sign makers, varnish specialists, wood workers, and artists all enjoy a camraderie whether playing guitars in a water-front band, having a pizza party or a passing tip of the hat. This is the heart of Sausalito's working waterfront.

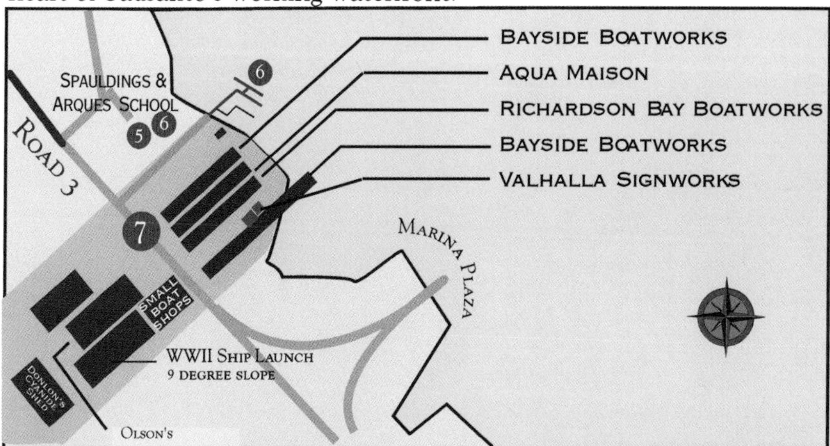

Enter the shipyard and immediately turn left and head for the gate leading to the marina. Follow the walkway straight to the end and then down the ramp. You will see the Arques collection of wooden boats directly in front of you.

San Francisco Gillnetter

This green and white boat is historically the most important boat in the Arques School collection. It is the missing link between the European felucca and the Monterey fishing boat. When the Mediterranean fisherman immigrated here, they modified the felucca design for ocean fishing. When gill netting became illegal, the masts were removed and a cabin was installed with a Hick's engine inside, creating the Monterey fishing boat.

Black Cat

Designed by Robert Darr, the Black Cat *is a 15-foot long open catboat built with lapstrake planking copper fastened to oak frames. Her pepperwood transom is curved and raked, and her sheer is high at the bow with just a touch of tumblehome—fast and beautiful!*

Michael Bush

In 1997, the Arques School sent a small team to Nova Scotia, Canada to measure and record one of the last of the Bush Island double-enders. Carvel planked over oak frames with several hundred pounds of ballast, this 2002 replica utilizes an original 1913 engine.

J.A. Linderman

The completed J.A. Linderman *is the star of the 2004 boat show at Jack London Square.*

"The late model Kingston Lobster Boat is one of the finest examples of the well-developed aesthetic sensibilities of American boat builders of the late 19th and early 20th centuries," says Darr. Features such as hollow garboards, which flow into a raked, curved transom with strong tumblehome and strong hollow at the waterlines, make this design particularly demanding to build. The boat was named after the late John Linderman, a great boatbuilder who instilled in his apprentices the value of craftsmanship and inspired in his associates the desire to perfect their art. Launched in August 2003.

Directly across the dock from the Arques collection

Jerry Daly

This 1930 woody was used by the SF Marine Department of the San Francisco Chamber of Commerce to greet incoming cruise ships and advise visitors on where to spend their money. Beautifully restored by David Olson who likes to take his morning coffee en route to Angel Island.

Stay on the same dock and head south.

Alcyon

This Bird Boat (hull #7) was built at the Nunes Brothers Boat & Ways Co. in 1927. Alcyon *was once owned by Myron Spaulding and has been rebuilt (more than once!) by Richardson Bay Boatworks for its current owner Lee Caldwell.*

Roamer

This recently refurbished 1935 commercial wooden fishing boat has a 35hp Jimmy engine and houses two bunks and a stove. Her hull and deck are built of fir wood.

Finesse

This 1960 21-foot Treasure Island sloop was built by Lester Stone in Alameda, California. The hull is made of mahogany plywood with mahogany trim.

Go-Getter

This 75-foot 1923 lumber barge tug was built in Houghton, Washington. She is built entirely of Douglas fir, weighs 58 tons and has a double planked hull. During the longshoreman strikes in the 1930s, she developed a notorious reputation as a 'strike-breaker,' crossing the picket line at nearly every port between Seattle and Los Angeles. Curt Berlind has kept her looking sharp since 1997.

In 2009, Playboy TV's "Naked Happy Girls" invited the Sausalito Wooden Boat Tour aboard to provide a cultural overview of Sausalito.

Leave the outer docks and turn left just before the parking lot.

Driftwood

PAINTING BY CHARLOTTE BERTRAM

This 1959 Chris-Craft cabin cruiser is home and studio to Charlotte Bertram, the oldest daughter of Richard Bertram, once the largest yacht broker in the world. She acquired Driftwood *in 1986 and subsequently added the little house on the back. She loves the neighboring birds and captures them in her exquisite sumi ink paintings (shown here).*

Sausalito Shipyard & Marina (formallyArques)

Leave the docks and walk west past the offices of Parker Diving Service and Bayside Boatworks. Make a left on Road 3 (entrance road) and head south.

Aqua Maison

Here is where the floating homes and houseboats are built and renovated. Reinforced concrete is poured into forms creating a barge on which the new home is built. These barges act as foundations and also allow room for living and/or storage down below.

Bayside Boatworks

Bayside operates two of the original WWII ship ways. Here they haul out the San Francisco fireboats, ferryboats and other large vessels which cannot be lifted out of the water but must be pulled up on a 'car' using a rail and cable system.

Who's on the ways today? The Caito Brothers from Fort Bragg pulled in with a magnificent old fishing boat built in Sausalito by the Madden & Lewis Shipyard.

The 1916 Charles Van Damme *ferry-boat's paddle wheel and steam stack are being restored by Mike Linder, owner of Bayside Boatworks, through community donations of time, money and materials (www.charlesvandammeferry.org).*

Richardson Bay Boatworks & Ways

In 1986, Ross Sommer and Dale Goff founded Richardson Bay Boatworks. Previously this building, resting upon wooden skids, served as shop space for Ray Speck and also Kit Africa. It is one of the oldest wooden boat shops on the waterfront. Their staff of dedicated shipwrights have saved many of Sausalito's finest —from classic yachts to Bear Boats.

In 2013 Graham Wheelock completely restored Bear Boat #60 here. This is the last Bear built by the Nunes Brothers of Sausalito.

Foreman's Shed

This little building was once the foreman's shed from the Alameda shipyard. Metal loops on the roof allowed the shed to be picked up and moved as required.

Butterflute Studios

The old boat lettering shack has served as home to the Sausalito Wooden Boat Tour and Valhalla Signworks-Boat Lettering, Etc. since 2000. Look for the Swiss flag waterside behind the fence.

This was once the location of the Boat Builder's Cooperative, which generated a number of new wooden boats and hosted a score of renovations. This tradition has been carried on by local shipwrights over the decades. Here are samples of their work.

Jeff Reid's woodshop was attached to a WWII building where Marinship workers punched their time cards. Here is interior detail on the Rangeley Lake boat he built in 2010. This fly fishing vessel is for use in lakes and rivers and designed so that a person can stand up in the boat when they cast.

Northbay Boatworks

Shipwrights Anton Hottner and Holden Crane, both graduates of the Arques School, build customized traditional wooden boats. (www.NorthbayBoatworks.com).

Katie

This 7-foot Bill Gartside pram was designed and built by Jody Boyle as a yacht tender for Dan Jones' Apster *using fir planks, oak transom, and acacia keel.* Katie *is named after Jody's wife and is the first boat launched by* Northbay Boatworks.

Butterflute

This Shellback dingy was built by Anton Hottner in 2010 as a raffle prize for Galilee Harbor's Maritime Days. Victoria Colella was the lucky winner! The boat is shown here at the launch party in front of Butterflute Studios. Victoria gifted the boat to her two nephews, Daniel and Isaac who sail her out of the King Harbor Yacht Club in Los Angeles.

Gracenote

This new Belvedere double-ender design was created by Doug Gilmore and Anton Hottner. Built by Hottner and launched November 2014, she sports fir lapstrake planking fastened with copper rivets to black locust frames and topped off with teak rails. This is one of several wooden rowboats commissioned by Gilmore, an avid oarsman.

Charlie Merrill

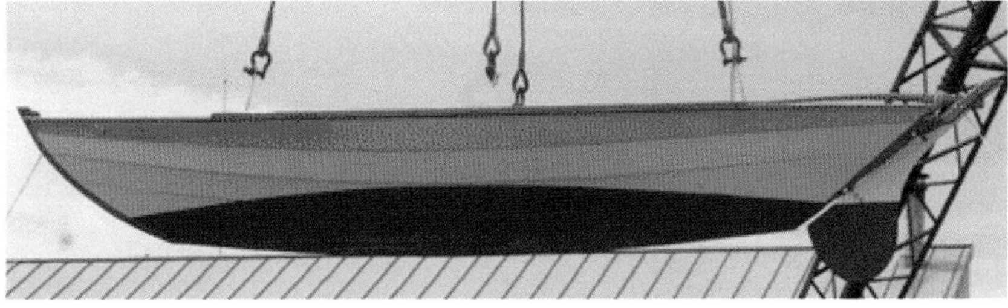

The Charlie Merrill *is a 17-foot sailing and rowing Swampscott Dory. Built by Anton Hottner under commission by the* Richardson Bay Maritime Association *to commemorate one of their founding members, the late Charlie Merrill. She is shown here at Spaulding Boatworks suspended in midair and about to be "splashed" for the first time.*

After leaving Northbay Boatworks, make a right and follow the fence.

This sturdy cement structure was built as an extension to the original wooden WWII Liberty ship ways to accommodate the larger oilers and tankers. The ways slant at "nine degrees of declivity," which allowed the completed ships to slide into the water under their own weight.

SAUSALITO HISTORICAL SOCIETY

Notice the rails embedded in asphalt at the west end of this building. These are the gantry crane rails. The huge cranes carried the completed ship sections from the subassembly station on Road 3 to these shipways, where they were attached to the ship's keel. The building has served as shop space for the maritime community since the war.

Between the two cement launch ways is the Purdy market building from Redwood City, salvaged by Donlon Arques. It served as Donlon's "toy box," then later the Arques School and is now home for David Olson's collection of classic runabouts and exquisite antique cars.

Inside Olson's is Al Capone's 1938 yellow Packard. (Donlon would approve!)

Leave the Sausalito Shipyard and Marina through the south gate at the end of the dirt road and enter Marina Plaza Harbor.

A gentle marsh covers the WWII shipways and some of the old wood pilings poke through the coyote grass.

Hindeloopen

Hindeloopen translates as "galloping deer." This 1905 barge was built in Belgium for the North Sea and has a hull constructed of riveted black iron. She was used to evacuate troops at Dunkirk in WWII.

The Modern Sailing School and Club was established in 1983 and offers ASA certification programs to its meembers... and a lot of fun! (www.modernsailing.com)

What's happening inside the big white tent?

Head inland and look for the big white tent.

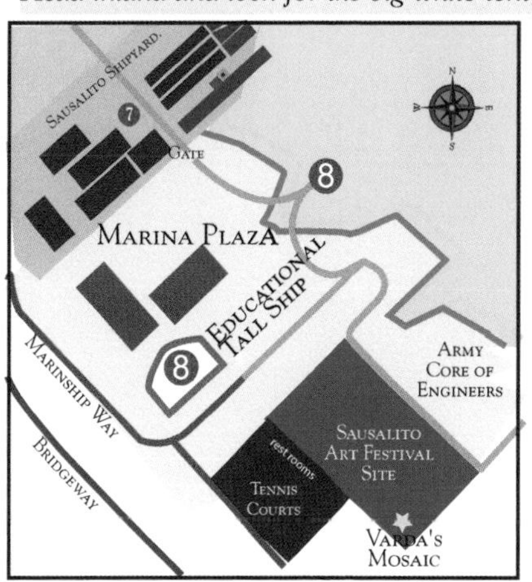

It took model maker John Ferguson 640 hours to build this scale model of the Matthew Turner. *The actual finished ship will be 132-feet overall.*

Matthew Turner was an innovative ship designer who built 228 vessels between 1868-1907. The Brigantine *Galilee* was his design and an inspiration for this project.

The use of a basic regenerative electric propulsion system makes this the Prius of tall ships. Instead of diesel engines, the ship is propelled by electric motors directly connected to the propeller shafts and drawing energy from large battery banks. When the ship is sailing, the energy of the passing water causes the propellers to rotate, which, in turn, causes the electric motors to become generators that recharge the batteries onboard. The faster the ship sails, the more energy is generated. The new ship will provide for an additional 12,000 students per year to experience educational programs in partnership with Call of the Sea.

The bones have been blessed and planking is proceeding on schedule for the 2016 launch of this magnificent vessel.

www.educationaltallship.org

Jean Varda's "Greek Wedding" mosaic is at the southwest corner of the Sausalito Art Festival site next to the tennis courts.

Head back towards the water and go right at the east edge of the green lawn. Behind the fence on your left is the U.S. Army Core of Engineers' yard where they crush up derelict boats and other objects found in the bay.

Bay Model Visitors Center

As its name indicates, herein is contained a scale model of the San Francisco Bay. The Bay Model also offers safe berth to visiting tall ships and sponsors ongoing educational programs such as sail training and marine research. Be sure to stop by and see their comprehensive WWII Marinship exhibit including a documentary film and artifacts (www.baymodel.org).

Sea Trek

Kayak and SUP rentals are available here in front of the Bay Model.

Seaward

This 1988, 82-foot classic staysail schooner is constructed of steel and was specifically designed by Russ Wooden for educational programs. Seaward *is owned and operated by Call of the Sea.*

Just south of the Bay Model, waterside.

Liberty Ship Marina–Antocelli's Pier

Originally the outfitting docks for the big ships, this pier was completely rebuilt by Frank Antocelli in the 1950s and utilized as Sea K Fish Dock where folks could buy fresh fish right off the boats. Now a marina, it also hosts several maritime businesses and seasonal herring fisherman. Two of the Farollon Clippers, *Mistress II* and *Ouessant* are also berthed here. (see page 62)

The entrance to the harbor is usually locked. With a little luck, a friendly local may open the gate. If not, you can view a few of the Bear Boats from shore.

Formally Clipper Yacht Harbor Basin 1 & 2, the Blue Water Yacht Harbor is now home to Blue Rush Aquatic Center where Stand Up Paddle (SUP) boards and oars will be available for rent. It is also home to a few of the famous Bear Boats.

The Bear Boats

The Bear Boat class was given its name by Cliff Smith, past president of the San Francisco Yacht Club, who commented, "That's a bear of a boat!"

In 1931, the *Merry Bear*, the first Bear boat designed and built by Ernest Nunes of the Nunes Brothers with his co-worker Marty Martinson, was launched off the coast of Hurricane Gulch in Sausalito.

The Bear class started off slowly, but by the 1950s was the largest one-design class in San Francisco Bay. Active and highly competitive racing continued through the 1960s. The last Bear Boat #66 was built in 1961 by Alameda Boatworks.

Puff

Puff, *a Bear Boat sloop, on display at the Wooden Boat Show at the Corrinthian Yacht Club*

MASTER MARINERS MEMBER PHOTO

Camembert 

Under sail and under wraps, this yellow-hulled Bear boat #57 was built by Bill Hines and rescued by Charlie Merrill and friends who found her sinking off Point Richmond.

A Couple of Happy Bear Boats–Juno & Magic 

Most likely you will find these 1950 vintage friends hanging out around the back fingers of E Dock. Magic was built by the Nunes Brothers in 1959.

On the road to Schoonmaker...

Before you enter Schoonmaker Point Marina you will pass through another area replete with maritime businesses. Inside the historic WWII buildings there are cabinet makers, wood craftsmen, sail makers, boat engine mechanics, welders, electrical engineers, and others involved in the maritime trades.

The WWII Machine Shop sits vacant awaiting its next reincarnation.

Follow Libertyship Way south, turning left just after List Marine sign and go onto the wooden boardwalk of Schoonmaker Point Marina, home to Sausalito's only sandy beach. Le Garage, and Open Water Rowing are the main draws and many of the charter boats disembark from this marina.

Yucca *(Down below left at bottom of first ramp off wood boardwalk) This 1937 Marconi-rig sloop was purchased in the 1960's by one of San Francisco Bay's most renowned helmsmen, Hank Easom, who has sailed her in hundreds of regattas and races. Easom sailed with Myron Spaulding when he was three years old and built many wooden boats here including strip-planked Dashers.*

Easom sails Yucca to win first in her class at the 2013 San Francisco Yacht Club Championship Series.

PHOTO BY LESLIE RICHTER

Legend (Kay)

This 1947 black hulled 47-foot yawl was designed by Sparkman & Stephens and built in Germany by the famous Abeking and Rasmussen shipyard. She sports mahogany planks over white oak frames with teak decking. Designed according to Cruising Club of America rules, she is very fast and has won many races.

Chorus

This Farallon Clipper is an ocean–going sloop designed to race in the warm waters of Southern California. *(see page 62)*

Gas Light

This is a replica of a 1874 50-foot scow schooner. There used to be a fleet of 400 scow schooners navigating San Francisco Bay carrying over-sized loads of hay. She is gaff-rigged with a flat-bottomoed steel hull and transom at both ends.

Gas Light *was designed and built in Sausalito by her owner, Captain Billy Martinelli, who sailed with actor Sterling Hayden and refers to* Gas Light *as an "18 wheeler of yesteryear" (www.schoonergaslight.com).*

Acania

Acania *is a 136-foot 1930 prohibition era luxury motor yacht built for the infamous gangster Al Capone. Designed by H.G. Wells and built by Consolidated Shipbuilding Corporation in New York, she has a steel hull and two new 600 horsepower Caterpillar engines. There were two* Acanias *built and this one was fully restored over a five year period by her current owner, David Olson. (www.acaniayacht.com)*

Apparition

This 1990s wooden hulled catamaran was designed to be safe, comfortable and fast. She was built in Sausalito at the now defunct Boat Builder's Coop inside of the Arques Shipyard by Stan Shiltz, owner and captain of Apparition *(www.sailapparition.com).*

Wanderer II

This 1931 schooner with fir planks over oak frames was designed and built by Lester Stone of Stone Boat Yard in Alameda, California. Inside is a plaque commemorating her presence at the opening of the Oakland Bay Bridge.

Follow this marsh past Tiki Junction and to the entrance of Galilee Harbor.

Between Schoonmaker and Galilee Harbor is the Mono Street marsh, which provides a glimpse of what Sausalito's shoreline looked like prior to WWII. Native plants are making a comeback, and at low tide, the hull of the Galilee *still can be seen. The totem pole was carved by Steve Weaver at Tiki Junction (around the bend).*

Galilee Harbor was named after the brigantine *Galilee*, which was considered a fast and lucky boat having completed 21 consecutive runs between San Francisco and Tahiti.

Two wheelhouses houses from the 1914 Issaquah Ferry *are now situated at either side of the main entrance to Galilee Harbor.*

Galilee Harbor is home to local artists and those actively engaged in the maritime trades. Historic vessels and "found-art" style floating homes sprinkle the docks. William Richardson once built boats here. During WWII, the navy built barges and afterward it was the site of several "live-aboard" boatyards. Sterling Hayden's boat *Wanderer* underwent renovation here before her famous flight to Tahiti, and Joe Tate's *Whitefin* was the last boat hauled out before the 300-ton marine railway and Bob's Boatyard were demolished in 1980.

The Galilee Harbor Community Association fought long and hard to preserve their way of life—and they won! They are now established as a cooperatively owned harbor, with their great spirit of solidarity and diversity intact. Galilee Harbor Maritime Day every August celebrates their victory (www.galileeharbor.org).

Community garden at Galilee follows in the tradition of using recycled and found items.

Guy Lombardo

Guy Lombardo *is the result of a Berkeley University student thesis. It incorporates a Buckminster Fuller tension roof, which was lifted by crane and placed atop a 1943 WWII Troop ship lifeboat.*

Thirty or more lifeboats were retrieved from the Troop ship *Oakland* berthed in Alameda and hauled over to Sausalito by Peter Bailey and friends in the 1970s.

Dragon Boat

Annie Hallat, a famous mask maker, once owned this boat which took 17 years to construct (1968-84)and includes found-art objects including Helena Rubenstein's chinoiserie porch doors. She is currently owned by Tom Hoover.

Mudlark

At the heart of this charming house-boat is a bird-watching station. Built in the early 1900s for the Audubon Society, she once floated in the marshlands of Richardson's Bay. She was converted to a houseboat by Peter Bailey in the 1970s and greatly embellished by her current owner.

Raven

This 1939 Mare Island military ferry, originally Heron, *was converted to a houseboat in the 1960's by Michael Raven known as "Stark Raven Mad."*

Delta Queen

Built in 1910 as a cook house barge for a river boat, Delta Queen *was converted to a houseboat in 1991 and is continually evolving under the care of her current owner and resident artist, Heather Wilcoxon.*

Rainbow

Ted and Ellen Stewart's houseboat has many special touches such as a hot tub inside the bow, solar panels, roof garden and an old wood burning stove. The hull was built in Taiwan in 1970.

Art Car

With so many wonderful artists at Galilee, there is no shortage of eye candy.

Galilee Harbor Community Association

The GHCA office is nestled between Galilee Harbor and Cass Marina.

13 CASS' MARINA AND DUNPHY PARK

Tucked between Galilee Harbor and the Sausalito Cruising Club

Cass' Marina was built by John and Mary Chalmers Gidley in 1961.

One weekend in 1961, John Chalmers Gidley, also known as Cass (short for Cassereno) and his friend Joe Tate, without proper permits, dredged this entire marina while the Sausalito City Council was out of town. When later confronted for their actions, Cass pleaded ignorance of the law and the City Council forgave them their trespasses. Cass and his wife Mary stayed, built a marina, and operated Cass' Rental Marina which was eventually sold to Bob and Lois Counts who ran it for 40 years.

On the south end of Cass' Marina, there is a little mound of dirt with a statue of a jockey holding a flag. This is where the dredging material was dumped. The Gidley family referred to it as "Do-Do" island. This area was also known as "Dredgetown" in the 1970s.

Cass Gidley Marina

Cass Gidley Marina–A Sausalito Community Boating Center

A new vision and partnership has emerged at Cass Marina. Teaming up with the Sausalito Park and Recreation Department, the mission of this young non-profit is, "to preserve a gathering place on Sausalito's unique waterfront to engage and educate the public about our rich maritime history and small craft heritage through affordable direct experience" (www.cassgidley.org).

The Cass Gidley Marina has been very successful in their fund raising efforts. They sponsor several yearly events including the popular *Sausalito Herring Festival.* Volunteers are rebuilding the marina and new docks were donated by the America's Cup Defender ORACLE TEAM USA.

Dunphy Park

This park area was used as a dumping ground until Earl Dunphy, the park's namesake, and Barry Hibbin, cofounder of the Richardson's Bay Maritime Association, initiated the cleanup and the creation of Dunphy Park. It is now the site for many of Sausalito's favorite celebrations. Friends of Dunphy Park are working to expand the park to include adjacent waterfront land to the south (www.dunphypark.org).

Sausalito Cruising Club

The Sausalito Cruising Club was founded in 1949 when a group of cruisers broke off from the Sausalito Yacht Club to form their own organization utilizing a wooden–hulled WWII munitions barge as their clubhouse. As it turned out, the water was too shallow to accommodate a fleet, and to this day, you don't have to own a boat to be a member of the club. The concrete barge bottom was installed in 1984. The SCC is host to numerous community and social events and features live music and dancing on a regular basis (www.sausalitocruisingclub.com).

The stream outlet just south of Dunphy Park is reported to still be home to spawning salmon and herring. No fishing is allowed. The area north of Dunphy Park was at one time a shallow estuary home for oysters and clams. But during World War II, the Bechtel Corporation dredged a deep channel to maneuver the big ships and the wildlife never recovered.

14 Sausalito Marine Ways

Follow the dirt path at the south end of the Dunphy park towards the water, through the open space, and enter Sausalito Marine Ways.

Here are the remnants of the old boat ways, now sprinkled with potted plants.

Sausalito Marine Ways

Boat builder Menotti Pasquinucci (known as SJoe Patch) built Monterey fishing boats here, picking up his lumber by horse and wagon. It is said that if you showed up with a sketch, he could build you a fishing boat in a few weeks! Menotti's son Frank followed in his footsteps but offered a wider selection of wooden boats.

Just west of Pasquinucci's was the Madden & Lewis Shipyard (1915-1960). Here they serviced rum-runners and Coast Guard boats alike. During WWII, they built subchasers, life boats, and launches for the war effort.

Shui-Jen of Taiohoe

This boat was built in the image of a Hong Kong Chinese junk. An "eye" peers out from her bow near the waterline.

Famiglia Santa (Holy Family)

Built in Sausalito by the Pascanucci brothers 1926, this Monterey-style 35-foot commercial fishing trawler was converted to an art studio and live aboard vessel in 2006.

Aurelia

This 1983 Su-Chow is a cross between a traditional junk and a hay barge. She was designed by Michael Bushbacher and built at Buck's Landing in San Rafael. Made from one mahogany tree, she has traveled to the Farallon Islands and back. She sports a lug rig and is finished with Marine Color, an oil based product used instead of varnish.

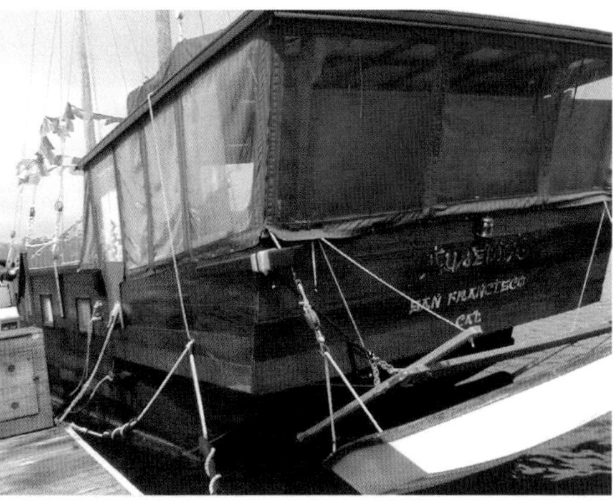

Aurelia *appeared in the film* Paradise Boat.

Mermaid Queen

This 1957 wooden hulled stern wheeler was custom built at the Richmond Boatworks. The strong hull is a combination of wood planks and plywood. A chevy truck gasoline engine powers the two paddle wheels which move the vessel along at up to 5 knots. Mermaid Queen *traveled under her own power from King Island Resort to Sausalito in 2014.*

Follow the boardwalk past the boat launch. Salito's Restaurant is the former location of Zacks, where the Mamas and the Papas performed their music. There were turtle races here every Friday night. Notice the old train tracks buried in the bike path along Bridgeway. The Bar Bocce building used to be referred to as "The Pine St. Station" and is believed to be part of the old train yard. Just south of it is Ark Row.

Ark Row

In the late 1800s, the first floating homes, the arks, made their appearance on San Francisco Bay. Kept safe during the winter months inside Belvedere Lagoon, they ventured into Richardson's Bay in the summertime. Arched ceilings, tongue and groove redwood walls and balconies all around are a few of the features of these landmark structures. Of the hundreds that existed, the few remaining were transferred to piers by 1917. By the 1980s, most of the arks were destroyed. Of the arks featured here, only one is an original—*Ark Caprice*.

Caprice (circa 1890s)

This is one of the oldest arks in Sausalito. It retains its original interior and wooden hull with towing irons on the backside, and has been owned and lovingly maintained by Marion Slater since the 1960s. In the 1980s, Marion witnessed the demolition of her neighboring arks (www.vrbo.com/7740).

Midway

R. Flower worked for J.H. Madden and built Midway *in 1929. She never floated and was Flower's tribute to the arks he so loved. The walls of the* Midway *are filled with rock salt.*

In winter, herring eggs are deposited on the support pilings under Ark Row.

J.H. Madden

This ark replica once belonged to fabled Sausalito Mayor J.H. Madden. Madden was elected mayor of Sausalito twice. The first time during prohibition, and his second term followed time in federal prison for working on a known rum-runner at the Madden & Lewis Shipyard. Ironically, the same shipyard was also working on the Coast Guard boats that used to catch the rum runners. Madden received a full pardon and was re-elected to become the most popular mayor of his era.

Bohemian

This adorable rendition of the 1918 ark that was once here, exaggerates the curvature of the classic ark roof line.

In the 1970's there were reports of mysterious sounds emanating from the arks. John McCosker of the California Academy of Sciences identified the mating call of a mudflat dwelling fish called a midshipman.

Julie Marlowe

This was the site of an 1917 ark, which was replaced with this charming interpretation in 1988. Named after the daughter of the current owner, John Wu (www.thearkjuliemarlowe.com).

R. Flower

Built by the Madden Family in 1987 and named after Ralph Flower, a long time Sausalito resident and shipwright.

Ark Angel

This lovely ark replica is home to local architect Don Olson.

From the arks, turn left toward the water. On the right is the Sausalito Yacht Harbor, left is Pelican Yacht Harbor.

Pelican Harbour

At one time only wooden sailing boats could berth here. While this is no longer the mandate, Pelican Harbour still hosts a magnificent collection of classic yachts and wooden sailboats.

NORTH DOCK *(Descend the ramp and turn left and then right.)*

Elizabeth Muir 

This knockabout schooner was designed by Eldridge McInnis in 1930 following the lines of the Eastward schooners. John Linderman and Babe Lamberdin started this weekend project in 1979. It took until 1991 to complete. She is planked with fir on oak, sports a teak deck and mahogany interior. She is fast, easy, and comfortable to sail and a spry regular in the Master Mariners' races.

Viking

This William Atkin design was built in 1956 for Rawley Kalagian. She has full-length mahogany planks over oak frames with a fiber-glassed plywood deck and ketch-cutter rig. She has sailed all over the South Pacific and Pacific Northwest.

These vessels are on located along the sidetie area of the north docks.

Tautira

This 1930 twin-engine Lake Union Cruiser was built by Viking Boat Works in Seattle, Washington to navigate the waterways of Puget Sound. It was once owned by director, King Vidor.

Tautira's current owner is Dana Hayden, son of film star Sterling Hayden. This boat was named *Tautira* after a province in Tahiti where Dana and his father spent a lot of time. The ship's bell from Sterling's boat *Wanderer* graces the port side of the cabin house.

Anna Lena

This is a Monk design built as a one-off power boat in 1951. Ed Monk, Sr.was one of the premier naval architects of the Pacific Northwest(1920s-1960s). He designed many vessels from dinghies to sailboats to power boats. Yet the Monk legend is connected more with classic power cruisers than with any other style of boat.

The Office

This Tiawanese fishing skiff know as a "piroque" was built in the Northwest out of marine ply-wood with an old-school Volvo outboard motor.

SOUTH DOCK

Double back on the dock towards the entrance of Pelican and turn south at the intersection to walk the South Dock.

Aqualeo

This is a 37-foot David Hillyard center cockpit ketch design. Built in the late 1950s, she is 37-feet long with mahogany planks over white oak frames. Her owner, Fritz Maytag. (Yes, that Maytag) .found her in Germany and brought her to Spaulding Boatworks where she underwent a four year restoration. Bella!

Serena 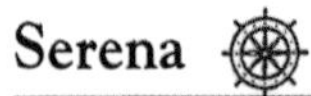

This 44-foot Island Clipper was designed by Mel Davis and built in 1946 by Fellows & Stewart in Wilmington, California. Sleek and sturdy with cedar planks over oak frames, her adventures include many trips to the Channel Islands. Currently owned by Jessica Brainard and local shipwright Jeffrey Reid.

Wanda (aka Wanderer)

Wanda is a 1963 44-foot Fishers Island Ketch designed by Henry Scheel, famous boat designer/builder and inventor of the Scheel Keel. All teak, Wanda was built by American Marine in Hong Kong. She is an elegant and stout lady, and very comfortable. She has been through the Panama canal twice and though very happy to call Sausalito home, thinks she might not be quite done with world traveling.

Sea Bird

This 1950 gaff-rigged Sea Bird yawl was built by Van Dmoll in Mill Valley, California. Infamous ex-harbor master Toni Marciante found Sea Bird in 1994 and restored her. Outside of one trip to Hawaii, Sea Bird has spent her entire life in the San Francisco Bay Area.

Thomas Fleming Day's purpose in designing the Sea Bird yawl class was to prove that small boats can be seaworthy. In 1901, he set off with two other sailors and crossed the Atlantic Ocean. Upon his return, he published the boat plans in *Rudder Magazine* and thousands were built.

Maramel

This 1929 54-foot wooden fishing schooner was designed by William Hand and built by Rancon Boat Yard in Seattle, Washington. She was acquired by Alan Olson in 1989, who traveled to the Pacific Rim and ran charters to Mexico. The boat has since changed hands and was converted from a gaff-rigged schooner to a staysail schooner.

Mahogany Fog

This 50-foot 1960 Chris-Craft Constellation has a modified deep V hull of mahogany planks over oak frames. Built in Pompano Beach, Florida, she spent most of her life in the Sacramento Delta.

Nancy Jane

Nancy Jane *is a 1925 classic raised-deck, carvel planked motor yacht. She was built with Port Orford cedar and Honduran mahogany —both now rare woods—at Stone Boat Yard in Alameda. She served as a rum-runner during prohibition.*

Vicar of Bray

This beauty is a strip-planked sloop with Bear Boat rigging. She has a flush deck with a wooden hull that has been fiberglassed. "Vicar of Bray" *refers to an old English folk song about a clever cleric who manages to survive the religious policies of five British monarchs by preaching whatever the monarchs wanted to hear.*

Peregrine

Built in 1929 by the Jensen Motor Boat Company in Seattle, Washington, *this 36-foot raised-decked motor yacht was designed by*Tony Jensen *in the style of a* Lake Union Dreamboat. *Her owner* Paul Donnelly *discovered charts aboard* Peregrine *dating back to the 1930s-1950s.* Peregrine *is a memeber of the* Classic Yacht Association.

After leaving Pelican Harbour, the first dock south is the beginning of the Sausalito Yacht Harbor.

Between Pelican and Sausalito Yacht Harbors, you can see the remains of the 1917 Lassen coastwise lumber schooner who's final days were spent as home to Sausalito's bohemian art community (1930s-1960s).

Wooden Shoe

The Wooden Shoe *is floating in the background. She was one of the original structures dating back to the houseboat wars of the 1960s.*

Sausalito Yacht Harbor

Sausalito Yacht Harbor was founded in 1940 when three lumber schooners, *Lassen*, *Wesley*, and *Santa Barbara*, once used to transport redwood from the Oregon coast to San Francisco, were deemed unsuitable for their tasks, burned, filled with mud, and sunk. The last remaining boat of this class is *Wapama*, now berthed in the Port of Richmond awaiting restoration. The tower was once part of the steam-driven barge used to build the marina, which currently is leased from the city of Sausalito by the Madden family.

NORTH BOARDWALK AND A DOCK

D.J.Arques

Scott Diamond's WWII Balloon Barge was named for his ex-landlord who built barges here. The Balloon Barges, built to fend off attacking Japanese aircraft, were never challanged. In fact, the only Japanese attack on the coast of California was submarine fire aimed at an oil rig in Santa Barbara.

Continue along the walkway, turn right and then left onto Row 800.

Spellbound

This is a 1960 43-foot Stephens flush-deck motor yacht.

These high-quality classics have stood the test of time, and we have quite a few still with us in Sausalito.

Taj Mahal

A miniature version of the Taj Mahal in India, this floating home was built by Emporium store owner, Prentice Hale, who then sold it to Hallmark Cards. Bill Havlan owned her for several years and, like her predecessors, her current owner spares no expense. The interior boasts of an elevator, wine cellar, and mirrored walls.

Flirt

This is a 1914 Charles Mower designed 33-foot sloop. Built by Ralph Flowers when he was a teenager on Mare Island, California, she won her class in the annual Master Mariners Regatta on numerous occasions. She was refitted from a center-boarder to a keel boat in 1928. Seventy years later, Peter Strietman found her deteriorated hulk of a body and spent one-and-a-half years rebuilding her even though only five percent was salvageable. A beautifully restored Flirt *was launched in the Arques Marina in Sausalito in December 2002.*

Ole

This 1960 Lapworth 36 was built in Southern California for ocean and bay racing. She has a strip-planked hull of mahogany over oak frames. John Hamilton and Carol Lenard have owned her since the late 1970s, and she has been berthed in Sausalito since 2000.

Return to A Dock and turn left then onto Row 700

The Farallon Clippers

These popular 38-foot sloops were all built by the Stephen Brothers of Stockton between 1940-1962 and designed to be at home in the bay or the open ocean. All are built with Philippine Mahogany planks over white oak frames with bronze fasteners and iron ballasts and feature a fractional sloop rig and narrow beam for a faster racing performance. Most of them are still afloat and six of them call Sausalito home. *Hana* is currently being restored at Spauldings, *Mistress II* and *Ouessant* at Libertyship dock, *Debit* at Richardson's Bay Marina and *Chorus* at Schoonmacher. *(www.faralloneclippers.com)*

Patita II

Launched in 1940 Patita II has cruised the Pacific from Alaska to the Guatemalan boarder.

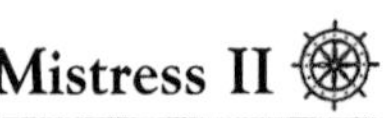

Mistress II

Built for Commodore Aldo Alessio, of the SFYC in 1955, she is currently owned by Jennifer Hinkel who founded Resilience Racing which provides rehabilitation for cancer survivors through the sailing experience. Currently berthed at Libertyship Marina. (www.resilienceracing.org)

Ouessant

1957 Ouessant is named after a French island. (once Goddess) She was T-boned in 2014 and underwent extension restoration. Now berthed at Libertyship Marina, she is also part of the Resilience Racing fleet.

ON THE BOARDWALK BETWEEN B AND C DOCKS

Cimba

Cimba *is a 1968 32-foot Grand Banks motor yacht. Built in Hong Kong, she is one of the last wooden hulled Grand Banks built as the company switched over to fiberglass when they relocated to Shanghai.* Cimba *was owned by Charlie Merrill from 1970-1990 and first volunteered for the Oceanic Society in a six year effort to clean up the San Francisco Bay. As a charter boat she made 65 trips to the Farallon Islands and several movies were filmed on her decks including,* A Whale For The Killing.

C DOCK

Rinta

This 50-foot classic motor yacht was designed by Edward Monk and built in Port Angeles by Edward D. White for Dr. Hay in 1938. Originally named Marilyn lll, *it is likely she was commandeered by the Navy in WWII. Two Caterpillar diesel engines provide 500 HP bringing her top speed up to14 knots. Her cabin and side decks are teak and her hull is cedar plank on oak frames.* Rinta's *inviting elegant interior beckons to another era. New owner and ice cream guru, Michael Lappert, brought this beauty to Sausalito in 2015.*

Adrianna

This vintage 42-foot 1956 bull-nosed Chris-Craft Constellation was originally built at the Chris-Craft yard in Michigan. She was completely refurbished in 2004 by the Ferrari Brothers, as evidenced by her gleaming mahogany hull. Adrianna *has called Sausalito home since 1984.*

Chris-Craft

Christopher Columbus Smith and his brother Henry built their first boat in 1874. In 1894, they began making internal combustion powered speedboats. In 1924, the first Chris-Craft appeared, a 26-foot boat capable of 35 mph. From 1924 until Christopher Smith died in 1939, they were producing 105 different models—utilities, cruisers and houseboats. Stellican, Ltd now owns the rights to the name and logo.

Encore (formerly Irene)

This immaculately restored 1966 39-foot Concordia yawl is the last of her type built. Mahogany over oak frames have kept her strong over the years. Her fourth owner, Bert Damner, brought her back to the racing circuit in 2014.

D DOCK

Sunda

The Sunda *was named by her second owner who developed the Sundameter, the first knot meter that could record boat speed down to 1/10th of a knot.*

This boat was designed in 1939 by Ben Seaborn and built by Blanchard Boat Company in Seattle, Washington in 1941. She is carvel-planked cedar on oak frames, bronze fastened, with a teak cabin, house and trim. She has a full lead keel with plywood for her bulkheads and decks. Her original sail plan was a fractional sloop rig with running backstays. However, it was changed in the 1950s to accomodate the lighter winds in Southern California. Sunda *won overall at the 1968 Newport-Ensenada Race. In 1998, Carl Schumacher reconfigured her sail plan to the original fractional slope rig.*

Spaulding 33' Sloop

Designed and built by Myron Spaulding for Sacramento Delta and San Francisco Bay sailing, this molded plywood sloop features a small spinnaker with a 7/8 rig. Cold molded plywood boats were very popular after WWII as the material was readily available, left behind by the military.

Valiant

This 1960 Sparkman & Stephens ocean- going sloop was built in Argentina with exotic hardwood planking.

Annabell *End of D Dock*

This Block Island Cow Horn was designed and built in 1993 by John Belinski in collaboration with naval architect, Al Vetter. Annabell's *skiff* Bat II *was built at Aeolas Boat Works in Davenport, California.*

The construction of this double-ended schooner served as Belinski's masters thesis from Antioch University and inspired four books. The original Cow Horns were larger open fishing boats with flush decks forward and removable washboards at the sides. *Annabell* has two same-sized spruce masts harvested from the Olympia National Forest in Washington. Handmade rivets and sails were used and the hull, made of rare Port Orford cedar, has been sheathed in copper. It took a little over four years to build *Annabell*.

E DOCK

La Jota

In WWII, La Jota *was commissioned by the Navy as an officer's "booze-cruise" between Tijuana and San Diego. She was painted gray and fitted for carrying torpedoes. At some point, she was lengthened 15 feet from her center.* La Jota *is a member of the Classic Yacht Association.*

Local lore has it that the 65-foot *La Jota* once belonged to Jack Benny. Originally designed in 1921 by a Frenchman named Mercer as a one-off design, *La Jota*, which in Spanish translates as "The Joker" or "The Clown," was supposedly named after Benny's writer. The writer was of Basque descent and *La Jota* is also a happy, traditional Basque dance. However, after further investigation through Benny's curator in Los Angeles, it was discovered neither he nor Benny's daughter had ever heard of *La Jota*. Yet another rumor has it that it was Benny's writer who owned the boat.

Marelia

Previously named Mistral, *this 65-foot Stephens motor yacht was built in 1973 and once donned the cover of* Architectural Digest, *the only yacht to ever have this honor.*

White Heron

This 1926 classic motor cruiser originally had a flat transom. The fan-tailed stern was added in 1938. Currently owned by famous Sausalito artist Jim Stitt, she is a member of the Classic Yacht Association.

Tiarona

This 104-foot Army LT (Large Tug) 2083 was built in the 1950s with a 1200 HP eight-cylinder Cooper Bessemer American-built engine. She has been beautifully refurbished and standing proud.

Sea Lark

This 1943 94-foot YTB WWII Navy tug was built in Seattle, Washington. She was originally named Pocahontas *as all Navy tugs were given native American Indian names. She was rebuilt by Thomas B. Crowley who founded the Red Stack Tug Boat Company in Oakland in 1893. Tug master, Harold Sommer ran her for eight years. New owners are working to save her for possible use as a Tugboat museum!.*

BOARDWALK BETWEEN E & F DOCKS

The Freda B

This 1980 80-foot steel hulled, gaff-rigged topsail schooner participates in the annual Great San Francisco Schooner Race. Freda B *was the name of Marina's grandmother, who worked as a welder in the WWII shipyards.*

Cimba *and* Freda B *are both owned by Paul Dines and Marina O'Neil of San Francisco Bay Adventures (www.sfbayadventures.com).*

Pursuit

A large racing sailboat, Pursuit *(formerly named* Avatar*), was designed by Burgess and Morgan in 1929 and built at the famous Abeking and Rasmussen shipyard in Germany. This is the last boat remaining in her M Class. This class of boat was created in response to the larger and more luxurious J Class, usually reserved for the very wealthy. Originally designed as a bare-bones racing yacht, this boat was never intended to have engines or any extra gear. All of this was added later. With a composite construction of wooden planks bolted to steel frames, these boats were created as expendable play toys to buy, use, and junk. After a proud racing history from 1948-1969, Ron McAnnan purchased* Pursuit *and has restored and maintained her ever since—a waterfront hero!*

Bounty

This 1950, 51-foot Sparkman & Stephens classic yawl is one of the finest examples of its type. Built at the Simms Brothers yacht yard in Dorchester, Mass. for both, racing and cruising, she was praised to be easy to handle as well as roomy. She is double planked with mahogany on oak and her big overhang leaves only a 34 foot waterline.

Coquette

Coquette *is a 45-foot mahogany planked, Stephen's flush-deck motor yacht. She was built in Stockton, California in 1966 and acquired by here current owner, Mark Cattell, in 1997. Her interior woodwork is finished with 25 coats of varnish!*

Stephens Brothers

Stephens Brothers Boatbuilders & Designers, Inc., was the most significant yacht builder on the West Coast, in business from 1902 through 1987 and producing about 1200 boats.

The company began in the back yard of Theodore and Robert Stephens. Over the years the company became famous for its elegantly designed pleasure craft, including sailboats, speed-boats, cruisers and private yachts. Stephens Bros. also built many vessels for the U.S. Navy, especially during World War II.

The company was sold in 1960, and the name was then changed to *Stephens Marine*. The yard was located at the foot of Yosemite Street, in downtown Stockton, California.

Today, Stephens Bros. boats are highly prized as collector's items. Stephens Bros. boat owners meet every year at the Stephens Rendezvous, organized by the Northern California Fleet of the Classic Yacht Association.

The Bird Boats –*The West Coast's Oldest One-Design Fleet*

Bird Boat owners will tell you, "Nothing sails like a bird." Designed to handle the blustery and choppy conditions of the San Francisco Bay, this class of day-sailors was very popular and affordable for the average person in the 1920s. Sausalito shipwright Herb Madden Sr., in collaboration with Clifford Smith, Sam Crocker, and John Alden helped design these 30-foot flush-deck sloops. The first Bird Boat, *Osprey*, was built by Madden & Lewis Shipyard in Sausalito in 1921. Twenty-four of these boats were built between 1921-1947. Their trade mark is a large main sail and small jib. Each boat is named after a different species of bird. Today the San Francisco Bird Boat Association governs the activities and events of this class, and they are found only on San Francisco Bay.

Since the closure of the "Bird Sanctuary" on F Dock in Sausalito Yacht Harbor, the collection of historic Bird Boats have been scattered. *Wigeon*, *Cuckoo*, and *Curlew* (owned by Bill Clausen) along with *Oriel* (owned by Dan & Linda McLean), have all moved to Richmond. Luckily we still have a few left on the end ties of E Dock, *Alcyon* is in the Arques Marina, and the *Mavis* at Clipper Yacht Harbor.

MASTER MARINERS MEMBER PHOTO

The Bird Boat Petral *races in the 2013 Master Mariners Benevolent Association's annual regatta.*

Petrel

One of the most famous Bird Boats (hull 28), she was built by United Shipyard of San Francisco in 1928. Pierre Josephs and Charter Kays found Petrel *in an advanced state of disrepair at an Oakland marina and restored the boat to her former glory in one year.*

Skylark

Built by Madden & Lewis (hull #6) in Sausalito in 1927, she was totally rebuilt with all cedar planks in 2000. Owners Peter Brosig & Jane Hook are now adding teak floorboards.

Kittiwake

This 1929 Bird Boat (hull #9) was given to Scotty McLean as a gift from his wife. Their son Jock McLean grew up sailing the boat with his father. She is now owned by Robert Fenner.

Some of the most famous boats on the waterfront are anchored offshore.

The first anchor-outs in Richardson's Bay made their appearance in the mid 1800s during the Gold Rush era. The miners arrived and filled our bay from shore to shore with their abandoned vessels. They ran for the gold and we ran for the boats. Living out there, off the grid, anchored-out, is a Richardson's Bay tradition. We host visiting boaters from all over the world. A small number of boats call Richardson's Bay their home. When they go their stories go with them and our waterfront becomes a little bit more generic. Sadly we have lost Ale Ekstrom and his 1942 navy crash boat, *Yesterday*. The 1917 Standard Oil tug, *Whitefin*, which stood testament to Sausalito's houseboat wars, is also gone. C'est la vie!

Ale Ekstrom R.I.P.

M.V. Suisun (aka Virginia S.)

This 86-foot, 1914 Army Core of Engineers survey motor cruiser built by the Wilson Brothers of Astoria Oregon has seen it all. She was as beautiful and luxurious as the finest private yachts of the day and charged with overseeing coastal projects such as the Panama Pacific Exposition of 1915 and the construction of the Carquinez Bridge. Suisun *was retired from government duty in 1931 and acquired by the owners of Safeway supermarkets and who renamed her* Virginia S.

In 1954 John Wayne and Lauren Bacall used the boat during the filming of "Blood Alley." Suisun *also hosted American and Russian astronauts from the Association of Space Explorers.*

John Speary acquired the boat in 1994 after it sank 3 times, had a fire, and someone was murdered trying to lay claim to the vessel. After 16 years in the Delta, John moved to Richardson's Bay. The winters have been a bit hard on her here and she is sorely in need of attention, but her thick 4" steamed white oak frames and cedar planks are keeping her afloat for now.

Teepee *(Anchored off South Forty Pier)*

Teepee or space ship? This innovative living space originally built in the 1970s has gone "green" with solar energy, providing the perfect dwelling for a local Apple computer guru.

Pronto II *(Anchored off Sausalito Shipyard & Marina)*

This 1914 custom racing yacht was commissioned by Frank Stone of the Stone Boat Yard in Belvedere, California as a college graduation present for his son Lester. She is extremely fast, and if raced today, predictions are that she would take the Master Mariners Regatta in her class. Thanks to the excellent care of Michael and Linda Davis, Pronto II *celebrated her 100th anniversary in 2014!*

Vadura *(Anchored off Schoonmaker Harbor)*

This 91-foot Alfred Mylne ketch was built in Scotland and spent many years as a magnificent charter boat in the Mediterranean and Caribbean. It is reported that she once had two grand pianos on board.

Floating Art Studio *(Anchored off of South Forty Pier)*

Larry Moyer passed away, but his floating art studio remains a sweet place to ponder and play.

Larry Moyer R.I.P.

Mount Eden

This replica of a 1920s stern wheeler was built by the assistant curator of the San Francisco Maritime Museum for use as a movie prop. These shallow draft vessels were used to move lumber on the Bay up until 1930. She sank in her berth in Sausalito Marineways and for now joins the ranks of the anchor-outs.

Marbara *(Anchored off Marina Plaza Harbor)*

This 1940 Rhodes 27' was designed by famous Naval architect Phillip Rhodes who described her as "lovely, comfortable, and nimble."

Marbara *was built at the Herman Lund Boat Yard in Erie, Pennsylvania with mahogany planks, steamed oak ribs and a Burmese teak deck. She features a "dog house" cabin and a whopping 54-foot mast of old growth spruce and a three-quarter sloop rig. The name* Marbara *means "a propensity towards generosity," and she has long been considered one of the sleekest anchor-outs in Sausalito.*

Sequestor (*Anchored off Schoonmacher Point Marina*)

Outside of a few trips to Mexico, this 1940 John Hanna Tahiti ketch spent most of her life in the Sacramento Delta and San Francisco Bay. She was one of two Tahities built side by side by Mr. Cups in Antioch who opted for husky double-sawn oak frames. Rebuilt by Greg Goble in 2000, she was passed on to her current owner Hans List in 2004.

Taihoa *races against* Sequestor *in the first Tahiti Ketch race on San Francisco Bay in October 2005.*

The Tahiti Ketch: "It's not a small boat, its a tiny ship."

Most probably more circumnavigations have been made in a Tahiti Ketch than any other boat ever designed. Boat designer John Hanna first introduced this design in 1926. Originally named *Neptune*, her design received little attention upon its debut. Twelve years later, Hanna's plans were published in *How to Build 20 Boats* magazine under the exotic name of Tahiti ketch. It captured the hearts of backyard builders worldwide and secured John Hanna's fame in yachting history. Now, over 70 years later, the Tahiti still has a reputation as a solid ocean-going vessel.

Herring Fisherman

Every year in January and February, the herring fishermen come in for the harvest. You know they are here when the harbor seals start making a lot of noise and the local chefs feature this delicacy on their menus.

If you visit Sausalito's downtown area, you will find adorable boutiques, world class dinning establishments, accomodations and views galore. Highlighted here are just a few of the more prominent waterside landmarks.

The Sausalito Yacht Club, adjacent to the ferry landing, was built in 1960.

Ferry Landing

The first ferry to disembark from this landing was the Princess *in 1868. This was a train terminal and car ferry hub until 1948. The switch was made from car ferry to commuter ferry in the 1950s.*

Yee Tock Chee Park *at the bottom of Princess Street is named after a beloved Sausalito merchant who generously extended credit to his customers in lean times.*

Vina Del Mar

Elephant sculptures flanking the park were salvaged from the 1915 Panama-Pacific International Exhibition in San Francisco and recast in 1936. The name is a reference to one of Sausalito's sister cities, Vina Del Mar, Chile.

Ice House

As the name implies, this was once the town's ice house. Later it was converted to office space by architect Michael Rex who donated the building to the city and, in turn, to the Sausalito Historical Society. Exhibits, books, maps and helpful docents greet and inform visitors about the history of Sausalito.

Scoma's Sausalito

This late 19th-Century Victorian was the site of a well-established tugboat and ferry service called Lange's Launches. In the 1940s, it became the raucous Tin Angel and, in 1951, it became a Sausalito favorite, the Glad Hand. Scoma's restaurant was established in 1969 with the merger of two Sicilian families, Scoma and Gotti. Both families have deep roots in the fishing and restaurant industry.

The Trident Restaurant

This was thee place to be in the 1960s-70s. Owned by The Kingston Trio, Janis Joplin had her own table here, and other musical dignitaries such as the Rolling Stones, Carlos Santana, Jerry Garcia, and Van Halen were regulars. Vince Giraldi played piano, and Robin Williams was the dishwasher. The psychedelic interior with its ceiling murals, and swirling woodwork are still in place today. The tripped-out menus have been made into posters so no one has to steal them anymore.

Valhalla (Walhalla)

Remnants of the Nunes Brothers Boat and Ways Co. can be seen waterside.

Once called Walhalla, Baby Face Nelson worked under-cover as a bartender here. In the 1950s, a famous San Francisco madam Sally Stanford moved in and changed the name to "Valhalla." When the Sausalito Woman's Club found out, they painted all of the curbs red so that Sally would have no place to park. In keeping with town spirit, Sausalito made her mayor! Sally held court in a barber's chair, and there was always a red light glowing upstairs.

Aft, After: toward the stern or back of the boat

Aloft: overhead

Backstay: a wire that supports the mast; runs from the top of the mast to the stern of the boat

Battens: stiffeners that fit into pockets sewn into the aft edge (leech) of a sail; stiffen the loose edge and provide more usable sail area and a better sail shape

Beam: width of the hull at its widest point

Boom: the horizontal spar that is attached to the mast at a right angle to support the bottom of the mainsail

Boom Vang: an adjustable rod or tackle that prevents the boom from lifting or dropping on deck

Bow: front of the boat

Catboat: simplest rig, with one mast and one sail

Centerboard: used in lieu of a fixed keel, a wood or metal fin that can be lowered vertically through the keel to prevent the boat from slipping sideways in the water, and can also be raised to reduce the boat's draft

Clew: back lower corner of a sail

Cutter: similar to a sloop in that there is only one mast, but it is stepped further aft and she can carry two headsails (forestaysail and jib) at once

Draft: the depth of water required to float a boat (can also refer to the fullness or roundness of a sail)

Foot: bottom edge of a sail

Fore: toward the front of the boat

Foretriangle: area in the sail plan in which the headsail fits

Genoa (Headsail): a large jib with an overlap aft of the mast

Halyard: line that attaches to the top of a sail and runs down to the bottom of the mast (can be internal or external of the mast)

Head: top corner of the sail (also refers to the toilet on a boat)

Headstay: wire running from the top of the mast to the boat and to which the jib is attached (The headstay supports the mast and prevents it from falling backwards.)

Hull: body of the boat exclusive of the masts (includes the bottom, topsides, buoyancy tanks and deck)

Jib (Headsail): a sail forward of the mast, attached to the forestay using jib hanks

Jib Sheet: consists of two lines connected to the clew of the jib and led along each side of the boat to the cockpit

Keel: major longitudinal part of a hull (also refers to a weighted fin or other member on the bottom of the hull that keeps the boat from slipping sideways in the water)

Ketch: similar to a yawl, it has two masts—the mainmast and a mizzen mast (the mizzen mast is generally stepped forward of the rudder post and the mizzen mast is generally larger than a yawl's mizzen)

Leech: back (trailing) edge of a sail

Leeward: away from the wind

Lifelines: plastic-coated wire rope surrounding the deck to prevent the crew from falling overboard

Luff: front (leading) edge of a sail (the luff of the mainsail attaches to the mast, and the luff of the jib attaches to the forestay)

Mainsail: the principal and most easily controlled sail of a boat (the fore edge is attached along the front of the mast, and the bottom edge is attached to the boom)

Mainsheet: line used to control lateral position and movement of the mainsail

Mast: vertical pole or spar that supports the sails and boom

Masthead: top of the mast

Port: left side of the boat as you face forward

Reefing: reducing sail area

Roller-furling: where a sail is wrapped around its leading edge or luff, similar to a window shade but vertical rather than horizontal

Rudder: flat surface at or near the stern that pivots about a vertical axis to steer the boat

Running Rigging: ropes (lines) that pull the sails up and adjust their shape (consists of halyards, mainsheet, jib sheets, topping lift, downhaul, outhaul, and cunningham)

Schooner: two-masted boat where the aftermost mast is the tallest or all masts are of equal height (can also have three and four-masted schooners)

Sheets: lines used to control a sail's lateral position and movement, as in jib-sheet and mainsheet

Shrouds (Sidestays): wires that run from the masthead to the sides of the boat to support the mast and prevent it from swaying

Sloop: boat rigged with one mast and two sails (main and headsail or jib)

Spinnaker (Chute): colorful, balloonlike sail that is used in downwind sailing (usually used in racing)

Standing Rigging: collection of wires that supports the mast (consists of the headstay, backstay, and shrouds)

Stern: back of the boat

Starboard: right side of the boat as you face forward

Tack: the forward lower corner of a sail

Tiller: wooden or metal steering arm attached directly do the rudderpost and used to turn the rudder

Topsides: sides of the hull between the waterline and the deck

Traveler: slide running across the boat and to which the lower block of the mainsheet is attached (used to change the trim of the mainsail by adjusting the slide position)

Trim: to haul in and tighten up on the sheet attached to a sail or its boom

Wheel: steering wheel used to turn the rudder on larger boats in lieu of a tiller.

Windward: toward the wind

Yawl: sailboat with two masts, the mainmast and the mizzen mast (The mizzen mast is usually stepped aft of the cockpit and the rudder post and carries a relatively small sail. Removal of the mizzen mast and its rigging will convert the boat into a sloop.)

Local Sausalito Marine Services

Aqua Maison	415.332.3910
Argo Rigging	415.331.1019
Arques School	415.331.7134
Atlantis Yacht Charters	415.332.0800
Bay Area Boat Works	415.331.3138
Bay Breeze Charters	800.849.9256
Bay Model	415.332.3871
Bayside Boatworks	415.332.5744
Blue Rush Boards	415.339-9112
Butterflute's Wedding Chapel	415.332.6608
Call of the Sea	415.331.3214
Clipper Yacht Harbor	415.332.3500
Club Nautique	415.332-8001
Canvas Works	415.331-6527
Cruising Club	415.383.8992
Dave's Diving Service	415.331.3612
Ferrari Boatwright Services	415.453.5051
Five Star Charters	415.332.7187
Floating Homes Association	415.332.1916
Galilee Harbor	415.332.4906
Gianola Canvas	415.332-3339
Inka Peterson	510.682.1044
H & M Marine Services	415-332-3507
Hans Rau — Custom Yacht Furnishings	510.693.9947
Johnson Hicks Marine	415.331.3166
Kappas Marina	415.332.5510
KKMI - Kaplan Marine	415.332.5564
List Marine Engines, Inc.	415.332.5778
Marina Plaza Harbor	415.332.4723
Modern Sailing School	800.995.1668
Anton Hottner— North Bay Boat Works	415.259.1830
Ocean Voyages	415.332.4681
Open Water Rowing	415.332.1091
Parker's Diving Service	415.331.0328
Pelican Yacht Harbour	415.332.0723
Richardson Bay Boatworks	415.331.0742
Richardson Bay Marina	415.332.5510
Sausalito Cruising Club	415.332.9349
Sausalito Marine Harbor	415.332.3100
Sausalito Shipyard & Marina	415.332.3552
Sausalito Waterfront Tours	415.331.8730
Sausalito Wooden Boat Tour	415.332.6608
Sausalito Yacht Club	415.332-7400
Sausalito Yacht Harbor	415.332.5000
Schoonmaker Harbor	415.331.5550
Sea Trek	415.488.1000
SF Bay Adventures	415.331.0444
South Beach Riggers	415.331.3400
Spaulding Center	415.332.3721
Starbuck Canvas	415.332.2509
Tideline Water Taxi	415.339.0916
Valhalla Signworks	415.332.6608
Waldo Point Harbor	415.331.3393
West Marine	415.332.0202

Victoria Colella is a native of New York City. In 1956, she and her family, Frank, Sally, and Frances Colella drove their Chevrolet across the USA all the way to Los Angeles. She studied fine arts and then commercial illustration and design at the Art Center College of Design, working her way through school as a technical illustrator at the Jet Propulsion Laboratory in Pasadena. After a two-year sabbatical in Switzerland, Victoria moved to San Francisco in 1978 and worked as an interior designer, graphic designer, illustrator and single mother.

In 1992, Victoria opened Butterflute Studios and introduced a line of children's educational toys including the award-winning *Color-Me House*, an intricate and sturdy corrugated cardboard doll house that children could decorate themselves..

In 2000, Victoria purchased the boat lettering shack in the heart of Sausalito's historic Marinship District and opened Valhalla Signworks - Boat Lettering, Etc. Here she found a unique community, learned the sign trade and developed her own style of painting. Victoria's Folk Art Collection is sprinkled throughout this book.

The Sausalito Wooden Boat Tour began quite by accident while helping a friend sell his 1940 John Hanna Tahiti ketch, *Sequestor*. Victoria published a website and created a phantom cultural event, the Sausalito Wooden Boat Tour, for the purpose of attracting the attention of the Internet search engines. Well, the strategy worked too well and Victoria began receiving calls from people who wanted to attend the tour! This launched her into the first publication of the *Sausalito Wooden Boat Tour* guide-book in 2003. Victoria has been leading walking and boating tours on the Sausalito waterfront ever since. TripAdvisor's Cetificate of Excellence was awarded to the Sausalito Wooden Boat Tour in 2011.

The Ropes
Cover and Page 22

Cover Art: Commissioned by Clipper Yacht Harbor, this painting illustrates the traditions of the sea being handed down from one generation to the next. Here tug captain, Harold Sommer shows his grandson, Andy, "The Ropes" aboard his tugboat, Alert. *In the background is* Sequestor.

Shannon's Angel Island
Page iii

Sausalito Yacht Club
Page 78

Final Days of the Wapama
Back Cover

Arques Morning
Page 27

Butterflute's Bayside Studio
Page 33

Trident Poster Art
Page 79

Vina del Mar
Page 78

Purchase these and other artworks by Victoria Colella at www.butterflute.com/art.

All photographs and illustrations in this publication are by Victoria Colella unless otherwise noted.

Sausalito Sea Chanty

In old Sausalito
on Richardson's Bay
treasures and secrets
you'll find here today

Fairy-tale people
of legend and lore
live in the boats
that sprinkle the shore

Row. Row bullies row
This "Little Willow"
has got us in tow

Otis sat here
and wrote *Dock of the Bay*
Varda he danced
with Nijinsky's Ballet

Kerouac and Watts
on *Vallejo* they stayed
Hayden on *Pirate*
on the *Ark*, Redlegs played

Row. Row bullies row
Those waterfront heroes
have got us in tow

In the World War II Shipyard
history lives— -
great things accomplished—
magic it is

Gate 5 to Napa—
Cranes to the docks
Seventy thousand
worked 'round the clock

Row. Row bullies row
Those Liberty ships
have got us in tow

Now the shipyards and boat shops
still humming today
Keeping' alive
our traditional ways

Restoring old *Freda*
Steaming oak ribs
Arques and Spaulding
gave what they could give

Row. Row bullies row
Those handsome young shipwrights
have got us in tow

At Galilee Harbor
battles were won
When they tore down Bob's Boatyard
it seemed they were done

But the Galilee crew
are a fierce fighting breed
and when the smoke cleared
their cove had been freed

Row. Row bullies row
Those Galilee pirates
have got us in tow

From the 1940s
artillery barge
you can see "Annie's Island"
It's not a mirage

Seems that one weekend
when the council was gone
Cass used his dredge
A Marina was born

Row. Row bullies row
The queen of the fleet
she has got us in tow

Now it's on to the fancy,
exotic and fair
Classic bright woodies
abound everywhere

There are Bird Boats, Bear Boats
Clippers and tugs
Monterey's, dories
all stuck in the mud

Row. Row bullies row
Those sweet varnish bunnies
have got us in tow

–Victoria Colella
Melody based on *Row Bullies Row*